*no. 18 in a series of research reports sponsored by the NCTE Committee on Research

D0048799

Language
*Development:

*Kindergarten through Grade Twelve

By WALTER LOBAN
University of California, Berkeley

National Council of Teachers of English
1111 Kenyon Road, Urbana, Illinois 61801

NCTE Stock Number: 26545

Library of Congress Cataloging in Publication Data

Loban, Walter.
    Language development.

    (Research report—National Council of Teachers of English ; no. 18)
      Bibliography: p.
      1. Children—Language. 2. Language arts.
3. English language—Study and teaching. I. Title.
II. Series: National Council of Teachers of English.
Research report ; no. 18.
PE1011.N295 no. 18 [LB1139.L3] 428'.007s [420'.7'1]
ISBN 0-8141-2654-5   76-41007

The research reported here was supported through the Cooperative Research Program of the Office of Education, United States Department of Health, Education, and Welfare, Project No. 7-0061, Contract No. OEC-4-7-070061-3102. This support continued through March of 1970. Since that time, Walter Loban has worked on this monograph as part of his responsibilities as a member of the University of California.

National Council of Teachers of English
Research Report No. 18

The first monograph in the current series of research reports sponsored by the NCTE Committee on Research was Walter Loban's *The Language of Elementary School Children* (1963). In that monograph, Professor Loban reported the data obtained from his analysis of language samples drawn from the same children at regular intervals during the seven-year period beginning in 1953. Although the scope of that longitudinal study would have distinguished it from all other studies of language development, it was distinguished even more by its pioneering efforts to develop new methods for analyzing children's language and by its contributions to knowledge about language development. A great deal of significant research on the language of school children has been done since that time, and most of it has been influenced in a positive way by Professor Loban's work.

As impressive as that study was (and is), it was actually a progress report. The present monograph is a continuation of the earlier study, following 211 of the original 338 subjects from kindergarten through the twelfth grade. Considering the mass of interesting data that could not be included in this report, "continuation" seems more appropriate than "final report." It is hoped that Professor Loban will find time to write additional reports based on his unique collection of data. This study is a monument to his fortunate foresight and scholarly patience. But it is a great deal more than a monument; it is a unique source of information about the structure of children's language at the various stages of development. Researchers, teachers, and students are deeply indebted to Professor Loban for this work.

Roy C. O'Donnell
For the NCTE Committee on Research

ACKNOWLEDGMENTS

Longitudinal research has its own peculiar challenges, each of them sufficiently overwhelming to the foolhardy as well as to the timid soul. Files begin to bulge with data, and the directions-to-pursue proliferate into endless vistas. Cassandras, Jeremiahs, and assorted Pitfall Finders spring up in an eternally luxuriant flow. The extent to which one wishes to abandon normal living emerges starkly and insistently from among the multitude of research questions. Time, the very virtue of a longitudinal design, develops into a tyrant threatening to obliterate all order and design.

When I began this study with 338 kindergarten children, my ambition and hope was to retain just 50 subjects until the end of 13 years, at which time they would have concluded their secondary education or abandoned school along the way. Most amazingly the study ended with 211 of the original 338, an outcome containing mixed rewards and punishments. Why such a remarkable retention? The explanation is two-fold: to avoid the all-too-common sample of affluent professional background, I relentlessly pursued those subjects whose parents were the least favored socially and economically; secondly, neither wealthy nor poor families deliberately abandon the gratifications of Bay Area living.

At first I used my own resources to begin the research, and I did the work alone. Later the University of California provided a small sum from its research budget, and I hired some part-time help. Then, as the data began to accumulate rapidly and the United States Office of Education began to support such research, the right person to dispel impending chaos appeared just in time— Mrs. Marilyn Williams. Her wise administrative ability and incisive mind tolerated no confusion for the remainder of the work. When her husband, Arthur Williams, added his statistical expertise and careful logic, the formidable project was under control. I am deeply indebted to both of them for their generous involvement in all aspects of the research.

It is difficult to determine an order of contribution for the other workers on the project, and I must do what dictionary-makers are forced to do when a word's pronunciation is equally distributed among several variations. Someone must be listed next, and so it will be Dr. Catharine Bullard, whose impressive scholarship dissolved the tangles of difficult grammatical analyses and whose humor, tinged with Missourian skepticism, rescued us from gloomy and rash decisions. Miss Janice Kujawa, versatile and swift, participated in every aspect of the research. Nothing was ever too difficult for her, but her greatest achievement was the sensitivity and courtesy with which she handled human relationships—with the children in the study, their parents, their teachers, and those of us who worked with her. Two scholars, John Dennis and Francis Hubbard, developed a method of applying transformational grammar to our oral data and took an interest in our entire study. Mrs. Gertrude Funkhauser, the secretary in our division of the University of California, protected us from casually curious questioners and handled all telephone and mail inquiries with her personal style of elegance and graciousness.

During the last six years of the study, the United States Office of Education provided the funds we requested. Dr. Doris Gunderson of that office took a personal interest in our work, providing many valuable insights. Someone whom we never saw, a gentleman with the jaunty name of Monte Penny, dealt with us by telephone; inevitably he knew everything about our research, always had solutions for our puzzles, and was humanly supportive both in warmth of voice and in the swiftness with which he eliminated barriers and hindrances. If the government had more human beings like Doris Gunderson and Monte Penny, "bureaucratic inefficiency" would not be one of the charges against Washington.

Over the years many other secretaries and analysts changed to such an extent that all of them cannot be listed, but to them I express my sincere appreciation. They became aware, as did all of us, that language is so complex, so flexible, and so incredibly versatile that anyone working with it, trying to distill something valuable from studying it, has a tiger by the tail.

TABLE OF CONTENTS

LIST OF TABLES

LIST OF FIGURES

LIST OF FIGURES

CHAPTER ONE

OVERVIEW OF THE RESEARCH

Background of the Longitudinal Study

The research reported in this monograph concerns the stages and growth of children's language in all the school grades from kindergarten through grade twelve. The same children were studied as they progressed through school during these thirteen years. It was a longitudinal study initiated in 1953 with kindergarten pupils carefully selected as a representative cross section of children then entering the public school system of Oakland, California. In the ensuing years, each of the initial 338 subjects remaining within a geographic limit of 100 miles was studied on an annual basis. During the last half of each year, every subject was recorded on tape, and data was gathered on reading, writing, listening and other facets of language behavior. The accumulation of data continued until the 211 subjects remaining in the study had either graduated from high school or were eighteen years of age.

Four of this investigator's earlier publications report findings on the same subjects and data for the period of kindergarten through grades seven, eight, and nine.[1] The present monograph continues to report on some of the same questions, but it also turns to new questions about language, questions emerging from the work of the earlier studies.

Purpose of the Investigation

From the outset, the basic purpose of this research has been to accumulate longitudinal data on important aspects of language behavior, gathering the information in situations identical for each subject and using a cross section of children from a typical American city so that the findings could be generalized to any large urban population in twentieth-century America. The major questions forming the purposes and dimensions of the investigation were:

---

[1]Footnotes begin on page 135.

- What are the differences between pupils who rank high in proficiency with language and those who rank low? What is typical proficiency for subjects at each grade level?

- Does growth in children's language follow a predictable sequence?

- Can definite stages of language development be identified?

- Can the velocity and relative yearly growth in language ability be ascertained and predicted precisely?

In addition, the investigation was also concerned with developing methods of analysis to aid the study of children's language and to locate significant language features worthy of further study. Such methods of analysis should make it possible to study the use of language in both its semantic and structural aspects. As the findings of the investigation were sifted and subjected to further forms of analysis, initial methods were refined or improved upon. Thus, as in any study intended to chart new ground over an extended period of time, the research was based on a developmental design with hypotheses and methods subject to modification during the course of the research.

The Subjects

One crucial aspect of this research was the choice of a true cross section of the larger population. Care was taken to select a proportional representation of the socioeconomic backgrounds typical of the city of Oakland. The family status ranged from those in definitely poor economic circumstances, mostly living in the industrial areas by the Bay, through the middle-class areas of the city, to those in the more favored socioeconomic circumstances of the hilltop districts. It should be noted, however, that stratification was not tied to a single variable. Precautions were taken to avoid any unique or unusual factors of selection. The four characteristics decided upon—sex, ethnic background, socioeconomic status, and spread of intellectual ability[2]—were chosen as the basis of selection inasmuch as previous studies of children's language identified one or more of these four variables as having an influence on language behavior.

A second crucial aspect—one of particular importance in a longitudinal study—is the necessity of keeping the attrition rate within reasonable bounds. At the outset it was hoped that a sample size of 338 would enable the investigator to retain approximately 50 subjects on whom there would be complete data from kindergarten through grade twelve. However, a combination of good fortune and persistence in following low socioeconomic subjects made it possible to retain a remarkable total of 211 subjects throughout the entire thirteen-year period of study.

Use of Selected Groups Varying in Oral Language Ability

One aspect of the overall research design necessitating particular attention is our use of three special subgroups selected from the total sample. These consist of a group *high* in language ability, a group *low* in language ability, and a *random* group of subjects used to represent the total group. The prohibitive expenditure of time and money required to analyze the data on all 211 subjects led us to use a random sample of students. Thus, for the purpose of this monograph, the statistical data will often be presented for the High and Low groups (each with an N of 35), selected on the basis of a thirteen-year cumulative average of teachers' ratings,[3] and for the Random group (N= 35), selected by a table of random numbers.

Data Collected during the Longitudinal Study

Throughout the longitudinal study an effort was made to obtain as comprehensive a record as possible for each subject, not only on linguistic growth and behavior but also on other variables which might have influenced speaking, reading, writing, and listening. Thus, the present research draws on the following sources of data.

Annual oral interviews

In the spring of each year, every subject was interviewed individually and the responses were recorded on tape. In any given year the interviews were identical for all subjects, although the content of the interviews was altered periodically to allow for the maturing of the subjects. Typical of the early years were questions about games, playmates, and television; in later years the emphasis shifted to such items as parties attended, plans for the future, and the magazines, comics, or books read during that year.

Typed transcripts of the oral interviews

During the overall longitudinal study, the most expensive and time-consuming procedure was the typing and analysis of the subjects' oral interviews. There was an obvious need for precision, since these typed transcripts undoubtedly constitute the most valuable source of data collected during the thirteen-year period, and as a result many thousands of hours were devoted to this phase of the study by a group of highly trained typists working to transcribe the interviews accurately according to a detailed set of instructions. Thus, the present research draws upon approximately 3250 typed transcripts containing roughly 380,000 words of spoken language.

In order to procure *comparable* samples for each subject in the High, Low, and Random groups, thirty representative *oral* communication units per year were carefully selected for special forms of analysis. This selection was done for grades one through twelve, with each communication unit requiring a separate sheet for the analysis. In addition, a similar type of analysis was carried out for the written language of the High, Low, and Random groups. Thus the enormousness of the task precluded analysis on all 211 subjects.

Written compositions

Beginning in grade three, typical samples of the subjects' written language were secured on an annual basis (one composition per year). In grades ten, eleven, and twelve it was possible to secure two or more compositions per year for each subject. Therefore, in addition to the data on oral language, the present research draws on a longitudinal record of writing ability from grade three through grade twelve.

Reading tests

The data on reading ability consists of test scores on either the Stanford or California test of reading achievement—generally with two or more scores for each subject.

I.Q. tests

In grade two of the Oakland primary schools, the Kuhlman-Anderson Intelligence Test was administered to all pupils. The majority of students were tested again in grades four, five, or six using this same test. A relatively small percentage of students were tested still further in grades seven or eight. In cases where a discrepancy appeared between a pupil's score and the teacher's observations of the pupil's intellectual performance in class, further testing was carried out either with another form of the same test or with the individual Stanford-Binet Scale. As part of the data-gathering process, all I.Q. scores were obtained for every subject in the study.

Listening tests and ratings

In grades eight and nine and again in grades eleven and twelve, the STEP Test of Listening Ability was administered. In every year of the study there was also a teacher's rating on a five-point scale for listening.

Tests on the use of connectives

In grades five through twelve, a test of the ability to use connectives and conjunctive adverbs was administered to every subject. The test consisted of fifty sentence completions, the written response indicating whether or not the subject was able to use appropriately such words as *unless, however,* and *moreover.*

Teachers' ratings

In every year of the study each subject's teacher rated him or her on a specified series of language factors, with each factor scored on a five-point scale. Throughout the course of the research, the following features of oral language, each defined for the teacher, were included:

1. amount of language
2. quality of vocabulary
3. skill in communication
4. organization, purpose, and control of language
5. wealth of ideas
6. quality of listening

In addition, beginning in grade four, the teacher was also asked to rate the subject on quality of writing and on skill and proficiency in reading. Inasmuch as a cumulative average of teacher's ratings was the basis by which the investigator selected the subgroups for special study, the scale merits particular attention. A sample of the teacher's rating scale may be found in Appendix A. Thus, we have at least thirteen teachers' ratings per child. These ratings were averaged in order to select the thirty-five most proficient and the thirty-five least proficient subjects in language.

Book lists

In grades four through twelve, subjects were asked to list the books they had read during the previous year. The assumption, of course, is that the lists are incomplete, since even an adult of good intelligence would have difficulty in remembering every book he or she had read during the span of an entire year. Care was taken, however, to obtain as complete a record as possible; no subject turned in a blank list. For subjects who were poor readers or perhaps not able to write the titles of anything they had read, a staff member obtained the information orally and completed the book list. For those subjects whose reading ability was so poor or reading interest so meager that they had not read a single book during the previous year, information was obtained on their magazine or comic book reading in order to have some basis for determining their individual reading habits.

Other data

Among the other types of data accumulated during the longitudinal study were statements about the television programs the subjects watched, personality profiles, language questionnaires, records of school attendance, grades, and general state of health.

Hypotheses Being Studied

In looking at language, one asks a multiplicity of questions and puzzles over many issues. There are hundreds of hypotheses to test. Here we have tried to select those most valuable for understanding language behavior and development:

1. Predictable stages of growth on important features of language development will emerge.

2. The stages and velocity of language growth will not show a steady, even pattern. Instead, there will be spurts of growth followed by plateaus.

3. Subjects from above-average socioeconomic status will develop the resources of language earlier and to a greater proficiency than subjects from below-average socioeconomic status.

4. Subjects proficient in language will use more optional grammatical transformations in their sentence structures and will be more accurate in their obligatory grammatical transformations than those lacking in proficiency.

5. It will be possible to construct a weighted index of syntax elaboration, an index which will correlate highly with other measures of language competence. By elaboration we mean such syntactical features as adverbs, clauses, phrases, appositives, and so forth—the ways by which the basic subject and predicate are expanded.

6. Whenever possible, a subject with high language proficiency will more frequently use phrases or nonfinite constructions of all kinds in preference to subordinate clauses. This is a matter of economy; where fewer words will be as effective as many words, efficient speakers will use fewer words.

7. Subjects with high ability in language will use more adverbial clauses of cause, concession, and condition than subjects with low language ability.

8. Subjects with high language proficiency will use relational words (e.g., connectors such as *moreover, although, unless,* etc.) more frequently, accurately, and earlier than other subjects.

9. In speech, reading, writing, and listening, a strong positive correlation will be found. Only rarely will a subject show proficiency in one language art and lack of proficiency in a second language art. Such subjects merit special study.

10. By using a specified set of data for subjects in grades one, two and three, it will be possible to construct a method by which one may predict the language ability of those same subjects in grades ten, eleven, and twelve.

11. Subjects with high ability in language will use more verbs (including auxiliary verbs and nonfinite verbs) as a percentage of words per communication unit than will subjects with low language ability.

CHAPTER TWO

METHODS

General Statement on Methodology

Wherever appropriate, standard procedures of quantitative and statistical description have been used. Methods derived from other research are described and footnoted so one may easily locate the original study. New methods are discussed at length and illustrative examples provided. The methods used make it possible to present the status of the subjects' language at equally spaced periods of time, providing normative data for the total group of subjects as well as for the various subgroups used in the research.

Segmenting the Flow of Oral Language

After the taping of the subjects' oral language, transcripts of those tapes were typed. A critical problem in the research was devising an objective method for segmenting the flow of oral language. After carefully trying various approaches, the investigator settled upon the *communication unit* and the *maze* as the two methods of segmenting most suitable to the data. A third method, the *phonological unit*, was seldom used; basically it is the analysis of the subject's oral intonation pattern by which the analyst may double-check what has already been carried out, the segmentation of the transcript into communication units and mazes. The intonation pattern, or phonological unit, is useful when any uncertainty about the communication unit occurs. In Appendices B and C, the reader will find complete descriptions of our methods of segmentation.

The communication unit

The communication unit is the basic method of segmentation used in this research. By this method the typed transcripts of the subjects' oral interviews are processed for analysis. In addition, this method of segmentation—used also in the analysis of the subjects' written compositions—gives rise to one way of quantifying language development, the average number of words per communication unit.

8

The definition of the communication unit may be stated either semantically or structurally. In *semantic* terms it is what A. F. Watts described as "the natural linguistic unit . . . a group of words which cannot be further divided without the loss of their essential meaning."[1] Watts' definition proved difficult to apply; his "essential meaning" could not be defined with enough objectivity to enable analysts to agree on many utterances they encountered. As a consequence, the structural definition of *communication unit* adopted for this research became that of each independent clause with its modifiers.[2] Kellogg W. Hunt, studying children's writing, uses this same method of segmentation; in Hunt's research this unit has been termed a T-unit rather than a communication unit.[3]

As an illustration of what does or does not comprise a communication unit, a very simple example may be given. In terms of semantics, if one were to say "I know a boy with red hair," the words would constitute a single unit of communication. However, if the words "with red hair" had been omitted (chopped off, so to speak, by a different method of segmentation), the essential meaning of that particular unit of communication would have been changed. "I know a boy" does not mean the same thing as "I know a boy with red hair." Furthermore, the phrase "with red hair," left dangling by itself, becomes a fragment. However, if the utterance had been "I know a boy/and he has red hair"/, the method would require segmentation into *two* communication units because we have a compound sentence with two independent clauses (we count *and* with the second main clause).

In more complicated utterances, segmenting by meaning alone (semantics) offers too many opportunities for disagreement when several judges are segmenting the utterances. Therefore the segmentation devolves ultimately upon structure (each independent predication with all of its modifiers) double-checked whenever necessary by the intonation patterns of the human voice—pitch, stress, and pause. Thus, in all cases, the words comprising a communication unit will fall into one of the following three categories:

1. each independent grammatical predication

2. each answer to a question, provided that the answer lacks only the repetition of the question elements to satisfy the criterion of independent predication

3. each word such as "Yes" or "No" when given in answer to a question such as "Have you ever been sick?"

Categories 2 and 3 are only necessary in oral language; Hunt's T-unit is based upon written language so he does not need to deal with *answers to questions* and *yes* or *no*.   The following examples illustrate the method of tallying communication units. A slant line (/) marks the completion of each communication unit. Contractions of two words into one are counted as two words.

Examples of communication units:

Transcript of subject's actual language	Number of communication units	Number of words per unit
I'm going to get a boy 'cause		11
he hit me./ I'm going to beat	3	
him up and kick him in his nose/		13
and I'm going to get the girl, too./		9

The maze

Listening to the subjects' recorded interviews or reading the typed transcripts of their oral language, one cannot help but notice how frequently they become confused or tangled in words. In many respects this behavior in language resembles the physical behavior of someone trapped in a special maze, thrashing about in one direction or another, hesitating, making false starts, or needlessly retracing steps, until finally they either abandon their goal or find the path. On occasion the path is stumbled upon accidentally; on other occasions there is enough presence of mind to pause and, presumably, to use the process of reasoning. In this research these linguistic tangles have been termed *mazes.*[4]

To define it more precisely, a *maze* is a series of words (or initial parts of words), or unattached fragments which do not constitute a communication unit and are not necessary to the communication unit.

In studying the examples of mazes, one discovers that when a maze is removed from a communication unit, the *remaining* material always constitutes a straightforward, clearly recognizable unit of communication. The procedure in this research has been to mark the maze in red brackets and enter a red number on the subject's transcript (as shown by the circled numbers in the examples below). Then, as a derivative of the initial analysis, it is possible to compute such data as average words per maze and maze words as a percentage of total words in order to have some measure of the subject's degree of linguistic uncertainty.

Examples of mazes:

Transcript of subject's actual language	Description of maze	Number of communication units	Number of words per unit
1. [I'm going] . . . I'm going to build a flying saucer/ but I can't think how yet./	Short maze at the beginning of a communication unit and integrally related to that communication unit	2	③-8 7
2. When I was fixing ready to go home, my mother called me up in the house/ and [I, I, have to] I have to get my hair combed./	Short maze in the middle of a communication unit and integrally related to that communication unit.	2	16 1-④-7
3. 1 saw a hunter program last Sunday/ [and he, and snow time he had to have lot wah-h when he not too many dogs, he] . . . and that's all I think of that picture./	Long maze not immediately related to communication unit. The child apparently drops the idea he was trying to express, deeming it too complicated for his powers.	2	7 ⑱-9

Note: Mazes are in brackets. The number of words in a maze is circled.

Statistically, the problem of dealing with mazes would seem relatively slight. After counting the words in a maze, one presumably has a number which may be compared to any other number. In actual practice, however, mazes continue to be one of the more confusing variables encountered in this research. The examples shown are generally termed "textbook examples," with each clearly defined to assist the reader's comprehension of what has been studied.

In addition to the difficulties sometimes encountered in analysis, there is a further problem with mazes, pointing up the fact that one should not become totally dependent upon statistical measurement. Frequently a situation is encountered in which two subjects have an *equal proportion* of mazes; yet, when studying other measures of their language ability, it becomes obvious that the language skills of the subjects in question are inherently different. For example, a subject with a *low* maze count may be the type of person one would describe as thoughtful, reflective, and careful about speaking precisely. On the other hand, a low maze count could be associated with subjects classified as exceptionally *poor* in language ability, those who tend to speak in slow, short communication units, those who appear to have difficulty in verbalizing their ideas.

The opposite case is those who have a *high* proportion of mazes. Here again we may encounter two extremes of language ability. In one instance, a subject may be so eager to communicate that words tend to bubble forward too rapidly, producing a high incidence of mazes. In another case, a high maze count may be the result of disorganized thought—a lack of verbal control producing a constant series of hesitations and false starts.

Dependent Clauses: Method of Analysis

All speakers and writers use many different strategies for elaborating their simple subjects and predicates, modifying not only through the use of adjectives and adverbs, but also prepositional phrases, appositives, infinitive phrases, infinitive clauses, and dependent clauses. This special study examines dependent adjectival, adverbial, and noun clauses; it then further divides adverbial clauses by *type* (such as condition, concession, or manner, etc.) and noun clauses by *function* (such as objective complement, direct object, or subject).

Subordination is typically a more mature and difficult form of syntactical structure than simple parallel statements connected by *and* or *but*. Furthermore, subordination makes possible a more coherent organization of related statements. Usually one thinks of dependent clauses when subordination is mentioned, but prepositional, participial, infinitive, and gerund phrases are also syntactical strategies for classifying thought relationships; through them, speakers communicate more complex propositions than are usually possible with simple independent clauses.

Some measure or index of subordination should reveal a difference between subjects proficient with language and those who are not. LaBrant was probably the first researcher to analyze subordination by a clearly defined series of rules.[5] She studied clauses as indications of skill in written language and developed a subordination index, dividing the number of subordinate clauses by the total number of clauses in each subject's writing. Thus her subordination index is the percentage of dependent clauses among all the clauses written by an individual. Her index does not take into account any subordinating accomplished by infinitives, participles, and gerunds, whether these nonfinite verbs be single or in phrases. In other words, her formula deals only with finite verbs and does not include the nonfinite verbs (infinitives, participles, gerunds) or any other subordinating syntactical methods such as prepositional phrases, nominative absolutes, and appositives. Following LaBrant several studies added to the body of knowledge on subordination.[6]

Another index of clausal subordination has emerged from the research of Kellogg Hunt.[7] This, too, is based upon writing and restricted to finite verbs, but it is computed differently. Hunt divides the number of main clauses plus subordinate clauses by the number of main clauses.

LaBrant	**Hunt**
Subordinate clauses	Subordinate plus main clauses
Subordinate plus main clauses	Main clauses

Neither of these indexes deals with nonfinite verbs or other methods of subordinating; at first, in this research, we also studied only clausal subordination, but this seems an unncessarily narrow concept of what subordinating actually is in human communication.

Thus ability to express natural or logical relations does not depend solely upon finite verbs. Analysis of proficient speakers and writers reveals skillful use of prepositional phrases, infinitives, appositives, gerunds, and other strategies of structure to compress ideas into more mature, meaningful forms. Therefore, valuable pioneering though it was, LaBrant's index of subordination remains an incomplete method of analyzing all the structural complexity used by speakers and writers for density and compression of thought. Mature speakers and writers also replace dependent clauses with phrases of all kinds, as in these examples:

Less Mature	More Mature
When Nina had fed the baby, she hurried after her father.	Having fed the baby, Nina hurried after her father. (Present perfect participial phrase)
Literature is written so that it can clarify the real world.	Literature is written to clarify the real world. (Infinitive phrase)
The dog was in such a wild fury that he bit his master.	In his wild fury the dog bit his master. (Prepositional phrase)

The function of clauses may also reveal degrees of proficiency in language. Templin found subjects age eight using five times as many subordinate clauses as subjects age three, but the difference varied according to type of clause:[8] the eight-year-old subjects used four times as many adverbial clauses, seven times as many noun clauses, and twelve times as many adjectival clauses. Evidently, frequent use of adjectival clauses belongs to a later stage of development.[9] Lawton's research also shows socioeconomic differences in the use of the adjectival clause at age twelve, but by age fifteen his working-class boys have caught up with the middle-class boys. "Noun clauses used as objects are very common and are learned early in life, but noun clauses used as nominals [subjects, complements, and appositives] are much later developments."[10]

Although clauses are often a less skillful syntactic strategy than verbal clusters in the *writing* of expert stylists, they do, nevertheless, prove to be a sign of language proficiency in the speech and writing of the subjects in this longitudinal study. In the early years of this study, the investigator devised a weighted index of subordination that permitted a limited place to nonfinite verbs. This index tallied all dependent clauses as follows:

1 point for each dependent clause (first-order dependent clauses)
2 points for any dependent clause modifying or within another dependent clause (second-order dependent clauses)
2 points for any dependent clause containing a verbal construction such as an infinitive, gerund, or participle
3 points for any dependent clause within or modifying another dependent clause which, in turn, is within or modifies another dependent clause (third-order dependent clauses).[11]

The reader should note that only if nonfinite verbs or verb phrases occurred *within* a dependent clause was any notice taken of them. Nonfinite verbal structures *outside* the dependent clause were ignored as were prepositional phrases, yet these are also a powerful structural means of subordinating ideas. Even so, this *limited* weighted index of subordination revealed that subjects high in language proficiency scored higher than a random group of subjects or a group low in language proficiency, and all three groups showed an increase on the index as chronological age increased. However, this particular index, because of the limitations described, needed to be replaced by a better index.

In England, Lawton became convinced by studies of social class differences in language that maturity of expression is marked not only by an increase in the frequency of use of subordinate clauses but also in the complexity of their structuring. He stated: "Several attempts have been made to measure this kind of complexity, and it was decided to employ Loban's weighted index of subordination, which has the merit of taking some nonfinite constructions into account as well as finite. The results . . . show clearly that the ability to use subordinations of greater complexity than the first order dependence may be an index of age development but that class differences are once again more important. . . . It is felt, however, that although important differences have been indicated, the measures used are linguistically very crude and are not a satisfactory method of carrying on investigations of any greater complexity. It would seem to be essential that future research in this field should be carried out using the methods of modern linguistics rather than trying to adapt the old-fashioned categories of conventional grammar."[12]

As a result of all these studies and Lawton's suggestions, two new methods of studying elaboration of syntax were devised for the present research. The first is a more comprehensive weighted index, including all strategies for elaborating a communication unit beyond the simple subject and predicate. The second method is the use of transformational grammar to assess subordination. Each of these methods will be discussed in turn on the next few pages.

Elaboration of Communication Units: Method of Analysis

In this research the *elaboration of language* has been defined as the use of various strategies of syntax through which the communication unit is expanded beyond a simple subject and predicate. Thus the study of elaboration deals not only with modification through adjectives, adverbs, and dependent clauses but also with prepositional phrases, infinitives, appositives, participles, and all other strategies of expansion.

In order to get *comparable* samples for each subject in the High, Low, and Random groups, thirty sequential *oral* communication units per year were carefully selected for analysis. This selection was done for each subject, grades one through twelve. In addition, a similar thirty units were selected from the *written* language of the High, Low, and Random groups. Thus the enormousness of the task precluded the analysis on all 211 subjects.[13]

The weight assigned to each elaborated structure was decided upon after an examination of the subjects' language.[14] The precise weights used in the research are shown in the list of Elaboration Index Weights. This elaboration index is a valuable insight into an individual's strategies in maneuvering language. However, it is complex and time-consuming and, as will be seen in Appendix E, it can be bypassed using evaluation designed to replace inadequate standardized tests. Other methods of analyzing and quantifying sentence elaboration have been described in recent articles on language. In the next section of this monograph we present another such method of analysis based upon transformational grammar. The analysis of syntactic density proposed by Endicott[15] is also based upon the number of grammatical transformations involved in producing a sentence. Another syntactic density score has been developed empirically by Golub.[16] These methods of examining sentence maturity have been reviewed by O'Donnell,[17] who concludes that the T-unit length (our communication unit) is "still the most useful and usable index of syntactic development over a large age-range."

A Transformational Method of Analysis

A second method of studying the subject's expansion of communication units was that of transformational grammar. Could this grammar reveal sentence complexity with more methodological precision than our Index? Complex sentences are generated from several source or kernel sentences. The matrix sentence, or independent clause, has embedded in it—grafted onto it—a number of other sentences. Particularly important is the fact that some transformations will require deletions, becoming participles or gerunds, for instance; they, too, must be counted just as is everything else that is nested into the main clause. We are especially interested in these embeddings into the matrix sentence, especially when deletions occur. It is our assumption that the ability to do this is a sign of the speaker's (or writer's) desire to coil thought more tightly, to avoid a waste of words in order to communicate more directly and effectively.[18] Professor John Dennis from Sonoma State University devised a method for our oral language, and Mr. Frances Hubbard, one of his graduate students, applied Professor Dennis's design to our data. It proved to be a valuable

Elaboration Index Weights

Language Variable	Points
Adjective	½
Adverb	½
Compounding	½
Auxiliary	½
Possessive	1
Determiner	1
Topic[a]	1
Frozen Language[b]	1
Parenthetical[c]	2
Nominative Absolute	2
Prepositional Phrase	2
Modal	2
Participle	2
Gerund	2
Infinitive	2
Objective Complement	3
Appositive	3
First-order Dependent Clause[d]	4
First-order Participial Phrase[d]	5
First-order Gerund Phrase[d]	5
First-order Infinitive Phrase[d]	5
First-order Infinitive Clause[d]	5

---

[a]Topic: instances of repeated subjects such as *The boy, he was in the street* or *I knew that the girl, she was my friend.*

[b]Frozen Language: idiomatic expressions such as *once upon a time, in other words, a couple of weeks ago, more or less, back and forth, a long time ago.* This was a vague category but, fortunately, few instances occurred.

[c]Parenthetical: structures inserted within a communication unit such as *I guess, I suppose, you might say, as it were, generally speaking.*

[d]Some subjects produce more complicated constructions, for instance, a dependent clause within a dependent clause. All dependent clauses and verbal phrases beyond first-order (second-order, third-order, etc.) received one additional point as the order of embedding increased. For example, a second-order dependent clause received five points; a second-order participial phrase received six points; a third-order infinitive clause received seven points, etc. These occurred very seldom.

approach but very likely too complex for use as an evaluation tool in the schools. John Dennis's design for oral language may be found in Appendix F.

Verbs: Method of Analysis

Every language is complex in some ways and simple in other ways: Polish and Finnish morphemes are difficult compared to Italian; the complex gender of German nouns astounds a Spanish learner. English is relatively simple except for its verb system, one of the most subtle and elaborate among Western languages. And in any language mastering the system of verbs is crucial to knowing and using that language. Therefore, quite intuitively, one senses that a study of English predication should reveal something useful. For instance, the authors of *Writing: Unit-Lessons in Composition* believe that the density—or proportion—of verbs in writing increases clarity.

> "Verb density" refers to the number of verbs or verbals as compared to the total number of words in the selection. Writing that has a *low* verb density contains too few verbs or verbals; writing that has a *high* verb density has a large number of verbs in relation to the total number of words. In general, the higher the ratio of verbs and verbals to the total number of words, the clearer the writing is likely to be.
>
> Computing verb density is not meant to be scientific. No mathematical formula can tell you exactly how clear a piece of writing is; your own judgment must give you that answer. Nevertheless, when you find that a piece of writing seems unclear, you will often discover that it has a low verb density. A low verb density results when there is only one verb or verbal for every nine or more words (1:9). A high verb density occurs when there is one verb for every five to eight words (1:5 to 1:8). The value of this formula is that it gives you the means to check the verb density of a passage *after* you sense a vagueness, awkwardness or confusion in the writing.[19]

Another aspect of the verb, one not studied in this research, is lexical. Do those subjects with power over language use more vivid, unusual, and precise verbs than those who lack language skill? For instance, the following contrasts:

The boys *went* down to the lagoon to swim.
The boys *streaked* down to the lagoon to swim.

He *went* across the street.
He *ambled (lurched, strode, shuffled)* across the street.

This seems an important study for the future. Because such research is time-consuming, no attempt was made in this project to
determine this development of verbs. However, it was feasible to
make a count of verbs and verbals. We felt that subjects who used
language with power might use more expanded verb forms such as
auxiliaries (would, will have been, might) and catenatives (had
been trying to operate). In one study of written English using
modern plays, novels, nonfiction, and periodicals, the use of expanded verb forms proved less common than supposed; only 211
verb forms out of 4800 were expanded forms, but we were hopeful
of getting different results.[20]

The present research deals with verb forms in the oral and written language of children and adolescents; our special study of
verbs examines, first, verb expansion or density and second, finite
and nonfinite verbs used in both dependent and independent
clauses. A finite verb is one requiring a subject and capable of
taking a subject from this list: *it, I, we, you, he, she, they.* Finite
verbs are those that may occur as the only verb forms in independent clauses. Nonfinite verbs (infinitives, participles, gerunds)
occur only if there are, first of all, finite forms in independent
clauses.[21]

Limitations of the Methodology

In procuring spontaneous speech from children, the relationship
between child and adult is very important, often more so between
minority children and Caucasian adults. In this study, the main
researcher (Caucasian) spent the period of September 1 to February 1 of the kindergarten year playing with the children, helping
them with their classroom activities, and recording their voices
solely to accustom them to the use of tapes and to his presence. By
February the subjects were definitely at ease with him and the
idea of taping. Thus, their early tapes—kindergarten and grade
one—give every evidence of being natural spontaneous speech.
The same is true in grades two through twelve. Of course, children vary in fluency; the minority children range from fluent to
laconic, just as do the nonminority subjects. Later when the study
employed a black adult, an attractive and friendly young woman,
no differences appeared in the response of the black subjects
when compared with their previous language recorded by a white
adult.

It is very likely true that in a school situation and with an adult,
some children shift the register of their speech, their usage, to
some degree. This was one of the limitations of a study of this

kind, a limitation accepted from the beginning. However, deliberate control of one's oral language is not easy and, over thirteen years of taping, the personality and natural manner of talking for each of these 211 subjects do come through loud and clear.

CHAPTER THREE

STATISTICAL DESCRIPTION OF THE SAMPLE

For purposes of this monograph the statistical description of the sample will be limited to the High, Low, and Random groups (each N = 35).

To determine the socioeconomic status of each subject in the research, the occupations of both parents (or legal guardians) were determined.[1] These occupations were then classified according to the *Minnesota Scale for Paternal Occupations*.[2] Once this was accomplished, each subject fell into one of the seven major socioeconomic categories comprising the *Minnesota Scale*:

    I. Professional
    II. Semiprofessional and managerial
    III. Clerical, skilled trades, and retail business
    IV. (The Minnesota Scale reserves this category for all farmers)
    V. Semiskilled occupations, minor clerical positions, and minor business
    VI. Slightly skilled trades and other occupations requiring little training or ability
    VII. Day laborers of all classes (and families whose sole livelihood was public assistance)

Note that even though the present study is an all-urban sample, some subjects fall into category IV, since the socioeconomic ratings reflect the *average of both parents' occupations*.[3]

Table 1 presents the socioeconomic data by sex and ethnic background for the High, Low, and Random groups. There is a high correlation between high socioeconomic status and entry into the High group, and low socioeconomic status and entry into the Low group. In reference to I.Q. scores, the same obvious generalization holds true, with high I.Q. scores centered in the High group and low I.Q. scores in the Low group. As we would expect, the Random group has a median I.Q. of 100. (See Table 2.)

Our subjects fell into three ethnic groups: Caucasian (including Mexican-American), black, and Oriental. Subjects from minority ethnic groups comprise a disproportionately low percentage of the

High group and a disproportionately high percentage of the Low group. On the other hand, the five black subjects in the High group show an ability to overcome language difficulties not required of their white counterparts in this research. And from this, as well as from the performance and ability of a number of other black subjects in the research, the investigator believes that the ways of studying the language abilities of black children are not fully developed in this research. We need more refined research measures to eliminate the pronounced cultural bias.

Table 1

Socioeconomic Status by Ethnic Group and Sex

High Group

Socioeconomic Status	I	II	III	IV	V	VI	VII	Total
Caucasian Male	7	2	4	1	2	0	0	16
Caucasian Female	3	5	3	0	0	0	0	11
Black Male	0	0	0	0	0	0	0	0
Black Female	0	0	0	2	3	0	0	5
Oriental Male	0	0	1	0	0	0	0	1
Oriental Female	0	0	0	0	2	0	0	2
Total	10	7	8	3	7	0	0	35

Random Group

	I	II	III	IV	V	VI	VII	Total
Caucasian Male	1	2	5	2	2	0	0	12
Caucasian Female	0	2	2	0	2	1	1	8
Black Male	0	0	0	1	1	1	0	3
Black Female	0	0	0	1	0	6	1	8
Oriental Male	0	0	1	0	1	0	0	2
Oriental Female	0	0	0	0	2	0	0	2
Total	1	4	8	4	8	8	2	35

Low Group

	I	II	III	IV	V	VI	VII	Total
Caucasian Male	0	4	1	1	1	0	0	7
Caucasian Female	0	0	0	1	1	2	0	4
Black Male	0	0	0	2	0	6	1	9
Black Female	0	0	0	0	4	7	0	11
Oriental Male	0	0	0	0	2	0	0	2
Oriental Female	0	0	0	0	2	0	0	2
Total	0	4	1	4	10	15	1	35

The real problem, however, is not ethnic minority status but socioeconomic status. This study will offer clear evidence that proficiency with language, as the schools and society view it, accompanies reasonable affluence. The subjects in this study who are impoverished in a socioeconomic sense did not perform well in language. They represent all groups in ethnic terms, Anglo as well as black, Chicano, and Asiatic. Social inequity, not ethnic background, accounts for the fact that a larger number of minority children classify as low in socioeconomic status and do not, in this study, measure high in language proficiency. Minority subjects who came from securely affluent home backgrounds did *not* show up in the low proficiency group. The problem is poverty, not ethnic affiliation.

Table 2

Kuhlman-Anderson I.Q. Scores

	Median	*Range*
High Group	116	99 to 133
Random Group	100	72 to 124
Low Group	88	68 to 107

Notes: For most subjects, there were available either two, three, or four separate Kuhlman-Anderson I.Q. scores. The *mean* was first calculated for *each* subject before the median scores were determined for the group.

Note that the median for the Random group fell at exactly 100, an additional confirmation of the validity of the selecting process. The I.Q. scores also supported the validity of the Watts vocabulary test of 100 items given in the kindergarten for purposes of selecting the sample.

CHAPTER FOUR

RESULTS OF THE INVESTIGATION

Basic Measures

Up to this point, we have described the purposes and methods used in this research. Now we will turn to the results, first treating basic measures such as words per communication unit. Then we will report the study of dependent clauses, the index of syntactical elaboration, the analysis of grammatical transformations, and the study of verbs.

We would like to remind the reader that we used three groups, each comprising 35 subjects, drawn from the 211 subjects for whom we have data spanning all thirteen years of the longitudinal study: High Language Proficiency Group, Low Language Proficiency Group, and a Random Group, selected from all 211 subjects.

Those 35 in the High group were, out of 211 subjects, the most effective users of language as viewed by all their teachers from kindergarten through grade twelve. Similarly, those 35 in the Low group were the least effective users of language over a period of thirteen years. Ratings of at least seven elementary teachers plus six or more secondary English teachers were averaged to determine these groups, thus ironing out any idiosyncratic teacher judgment. It seems important to note that the differences between these groups are consistent for all language features measured in this research. For instance the High group is high and the Low group is low in *all these attributes*:

- average number of words per communication unit
- syntactical elaboration of subject and predicate
- number of grammatical transformations (especially multiple-base deletion transformations)
- proportion of mazes to total speech
- reading ability
- writing ability
- height and range of vocabulary[1]

- scores on listening tests[2]
- use of connectors (*unless, although,* etc.)
- use of tentativeness: supposition, hypotheses, conditional statements (the Low Group is more inflexible, dogmatic, unwilling or unable to entertain nuances or ambiguity.)[3]
- number of dependent clauses
- use of adjectival clauses

The stability and consistency of these two groups on so many features of language is persuasive evidence that the Teachers' Rating does actually sort out the extremes in language proficiency.

For a third group of 35, to represent the total 211 subjects, we used a table of random numbers and drew whoever fell into the requirements of that technique. On all the measures this Random group falls neatly between the High and Low groups.

Fluency with oral language

Fluency with oral language generally connotes a readiness to express oneself combined with a smooth, easy flow of words, as frequently exemplified in the language of skilled public speakers. In the language of children, however, one cannot expect to find the same degree of proficiency. Even at the high school level, children obviously lack the polish and rhetorical skill of the trained public speaker; in examining their language one must search for less polished indications of their fluency, for evidence pertaining to their volume of language, length of communication units, and freedom from any language tangles. Three measures in this research bear upon this feature of fluency: the average number of words per communication unit, the number of words in mazes as a percent of total words, and the syntactical expansion of simple subject and predicate.

Average number of words per communication unit—oral language

A high average number of words per communication unit could simply be the result of verbosity—an increased use of language without any significant increase in meaningful communication. In this research, however, this has not proved to be the case. Almost without exception, a high average number of words per unit is accompanied by a high teacher's rating on language skill, by a more effective use of phrases and clauses, and by the increased use of other forms of elaboration contributing to clear and meaningful communication. For this reason the average number of words per communication unit has proved to be one of the most crucial measures of fluency developed during the course of the investigation.

The data. For each group the data on average number of words per communication unit indicate a relatively steady upward progression. (See Table 3 and Figure 1.) The lines on the graph in Figure 1 do not cross or even come close to crossing, and in grade twelve the High group exhibits virtually the same degree of superiority it showed in grade one. Thus, from the standpoint of obtaining a simple, straightforward method to measure the degree of fluency with language, the average number of words per communication unit appears to be an exceptionally good device. Note that the Low group does not even reach the High group's first-grade level until the Low group is in the fifth grade.

Stages and velocity. In average number of words per communication unit, stages of growth are most clearly discernible in the Random group. Virtually without exception, a year of growth is followed by a plateau and then by another year of growth (see Figure 1). Thus, the pattern for the Random group (the *typical* subject) appears to be one of a high velocity of growth followed by a consolidation; this is not typical of the High or Low group until grade eight.

Relative growth. The relative growth of the three groups is shown in Table 3. For this computation, we have used the Random group at grade twelve as 100% and have calculated in the same manner as the cost of living index or similar indices. These data are most valuable in that they enable one to see clearly percentage comparisons among the groups.

Prediction and crucial characteristics. Since this research is longitudinal, it is simultaneously descriptive and predictive. In other words, we know in advance exactly how a cross section of subjects did in fact perform throughout a twelve-year period, and from the accumulated data we can then predict how similar subjects in other urban areas will perform in a similar situation.

The most crucial characteristic pertaining to average words per unit is the huge difference in ability exhibited by the groups—a difference which does not appear remarkable from the graphic presentation but which becomes more obvious when one examines the statistical data in Table 3. In grade one, for example, the High group has an average of 7.91 words per communication unit; this level of achievement is not reached by the Low group until grade *five.* Similarly, the High group has an average of 10.32

Table 3

Average Number of Words Per Communication Unit—Oral Language

Grade	Average Number of Words per Communication Unit (mean)			Relative Growth[a] (in percent)			Year-to-Year Velocity[b] (in percent)		
	High Group	Random Group	Low Group	High Group	Random Group	Low Group	High Group	Random Group	Low Group
1	7.91	6.88	5.91	67.61	58.80	50.51	—	—	+6.33
2	8.10	7.56	6.65	69.23	64.62	56.84	+1.62	+ 5.82	+3.67
3	8.38	7.62	7.08	71.62	65.13	60.51	+2.39	+ 0.51	+4.02
4	9.28	9.00	7.55	79.32	76.92	64.53	+7.70	+11.79	+2.99
5	9.59	8.82	7.90	81.97	75.38	67.52	+2.65	− 1.54	+5.73
6	10.32	9.82	8.57	88.21	83.93	73.25	+6.24	+ 8.55	+3.76
7	11.14	9.75	9.01	95.21	83.33	77.01	+7.00	− 0.60	+4.36
8	11.59	10.71	9.52	99.06	91.54	81.37	+3.85	+ 8.21	+2.22
9	11.73	10.96	9.26	100.26	93.68	79.15	+1.20	+ 2.14	+1.28
10	12.34	10.68	9.41	105.47	91.28	80.43	+5.21	− 2.40	+6.58
11	13.00	11.17	10.18	111.11	95.47	87.01	+5.64	+ 4.19	+4.02
12	12.84	11.70	10.65	109.74	100.00	91.03	−1.37	+ 4.53	

[a]Relative Growth uses the scores of the Random group at grade twelve to equal 100 percent.
[b]Year-to-Year Velocity is the percentage change in any given group from one year to the following year.

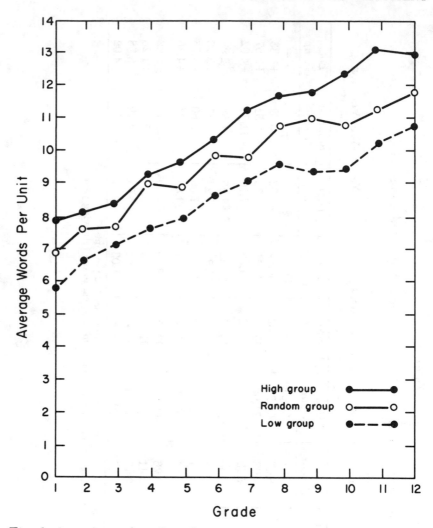

Fig. 1. Average number of words per communication unit—oral language (mean).

words per unit in grade six, while this is not equaled by the Low group until grade eleven or twelve. Large divergences between the High and Random or the Random and Low groups are also obvious. Therefore, as a generalization we may state that a High subject is approximately four or five years ahead of a Low subject and between one and three years ahead of a Random (typical) subject.

Words in mazes as a percentage of total words—oral language

Given as a percentage of total spoken words, the number of words in mazes is actually a simple and straightforward device for measuring the subjects' repetitions and language tangles. For example, if a subject had 450 words in communication units and 50 words in mazes, for a total of 500 words, the ratio would be 50:500, or 10% of all oral communications.

The first feature apparent from the data is that the High group consistently shows the smallest degree of maze behavior, with the Random and Low groups proportionately higher (see Table 4 and Figure 2). Also of interest—and this is especially true for the Low group although it also pertains to the High and Random groups— is the fact that erratic upward and downward fluctuations occur during the middle years of schooling (approximately grades four through nine or ten). A less obvious feature of the data—but perhaps the most crucial of all—is that *all* groups end in grade twelve with virtually the identical percentages with which they began in grade one. In other words, *all* subjects maintain their initial proportion of maze words to total words *despite the fact that increasing chronological age produces an increasing complexity in their language*. Could hesitation in language be a deep part of an individual's personality rather than an external feature amenable to education and development?

Table 4

Maze Words as a Percentage of Total Words—Oral Language

Grade	High Group	Random Group	Low Group
1	7.61	7.46	9.04
2	6.21	8.03	8.31
3	4.71	6.39	7.98
4	6.39	8.38	11.06
5	6.41	7.53	9.04
6	6.98	8.29	10.33
7	5.82	7.76	11.08
8	6.08	8.12	9.30
9	5.31	7.29	10.18
10	7.45	7.40	7.51
11	7.32	7.04	9.01
12	7.25	7.04	9.19

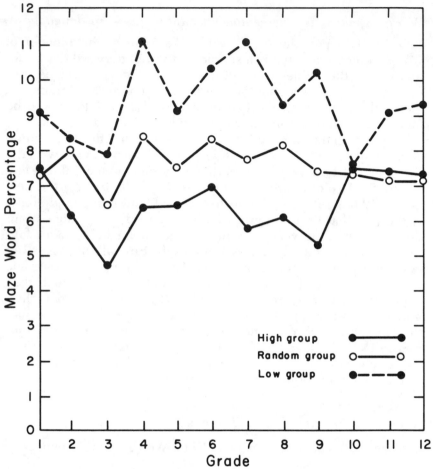

Fig. 2. Maze words as a percentage of total words—oral language.

Average number of words per maze—oral language

The average number of words per maze is the subject's total number of maze words divided by the total number of mazes. For example, a total of ten mazes and twenty maze words would produce an average of 2.00 words per maze.

This particular measure has a tendency to *understate* the Low group's difficulties in overcoming these obstacles to fluency (mazes) since the Low group uses a lower number of words per communication unit than either the High or Random group. From a purely logical standpoint, one would expect the probability of becoming tangled in language to be *disproportionately* low if a subject uses communication units of relatively short length. This measure is of interest because it emphasizes the fact that the High group consistently has a lower average number of words per maze than the Low group while simultaneously using a higher average number of words per communication unit (see Table 5 and Figure 3).

Table 5

Average Number of Words Per Maze—Oral Language
(mean)

Grade	High Group	Random Group	Low Group
1	1.94	2.09	1.81
2	1.89	1.89	1.90
3	1.88	1.85	1.98
4	1.97	2.06	1.99
5	1.93	2.09	2.07
6	2.15	2.21	2.16
7	1.90	2.06	2.17
8	1.96	2.01	2.11
9	1.78	1.98	2.18
10	1.85	1.92	1.92
11	1.94	1.97	1.97
12	1.77	1.99	2.24

Proficiency with Written Language

The findings on written language are based upon compositions obtained in the spring of each school year, grades three through twelve. To facilitate comparisons between the subjects' oral and written language, the findings will be presented side-by-side rather than in separate chapters.[4]

Average Number of Words per Communication Unit—Written Language

In written language, the average number of words per communication unit does not parallel the smooth development pattern found in oral language. (Compare Table 6 and Figure 4 with Table 3 and Figure 1). For all groups the writing curves are more erratic in the graphic presentation; large upward trends are generally followed by what apparently is not merely consolidation of growth but rather a downward shift. Our Random group is always slightly below the scores presented in the research of Hunt and O'Donnell, whose subjects present scores similar to our High group.[5]

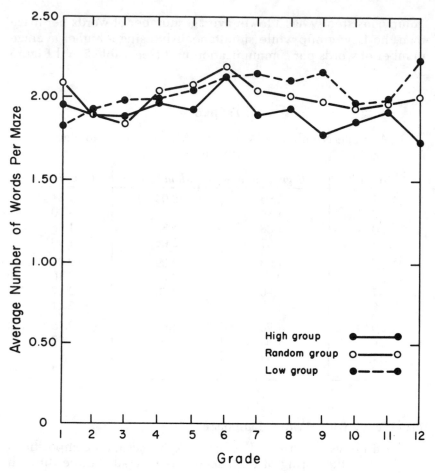

Fig. 3. Average number of words per maze—oral language (mean).

Despite the relatively erratic patterns on the graph, the High group is still obviously superior to the Low group by roughly the same margin found in oral language. All three groups show rapid growth in writing from grades nine to ten, but only the High and Random groups show another velocity surge from eleven to twelve. They are the ones who are anticipating a college education. Thus we can predict with relative assurance that on written language as well as on oral language a High subject will be approximately four or five years ahead of a Low subject in this aspect of language development. Again, the Random (typical) subject falls between the High and Low groups, and the curves do not cross except for what is apparently a minor quirk at grade eleven.[6]

Table 6

Average Number of Words per Communication Unit—Written Language

Grade	Average Number of Words per Communication Unit (mean)			Relative Growth[a] (in percent)			Year-to-Year Velocity[b] (in percent)		
	High Group	Random Group	Low Group	High Group	Random Group	Low Group	High Group	Random Group	Low Group
3	7.68	7.60	5.65	58	57	43	—	—	—
4	8.83	8.02	6.01	67	60	45	+ 9	+ 3	+ 2
5	9.52	8.76	6.29	72	66	47	+ 5	+ 6	+ 2
6	10.23	9.04	6.91	77	68	52	+ 5	+ 2	+ 5
7	10.83	8.94	7.52	82	67	57	+ 5	− 1	+ 5
8	11.24	10.37	9.49	85	78	72	+ 3	+11	+15
9	11.09	10.05	8.78	84	76	66	− 1	− 2	− 6
10	12.59	11.79	11.03	95	89	83	+11	+13	+17
11	11.82	10.69	11.21	89	81	84	− 6	− 8	+ 1
12	14.06	13.27	11.24	106	100	85	+17	+19	+ 1

[a]Relative Growth uses the Random group at grade twelve to equal 100 percent.
[b]Year-to-Year Velocity is the percentage change in any given group from one year to the following year. The impact of anticipating or not anticipating college apparently accounts for the velocities that emerge at grade twelve.

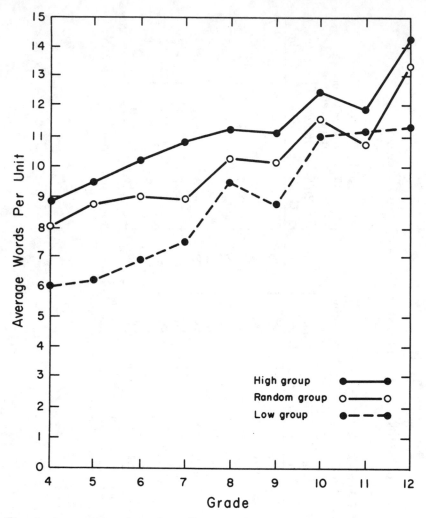

Fig. 4. Average number of words per communication unit—written language (mean).

Comparison of Oral and Written Language

One informative comparison arises by placing data on the oral and written average number of words per communication unit side-by-side on the same table (see Table 7). From this comparison, the reader can see that from grades one through seven the *oral* average words per unit tends to be slightly higher than the *written* average. In grades seven through nine a rapprochement seems to be occurring, and in grades ten through twelve longer units occur in writing.

Table 7

Average Number of Words Per Communication Unit—
Comparison of Oral and Written Language
(mean)

Grade	High Group		Random Group		Low Group	
	Oral	Written	Oral	Written	Oral	Written
1	7.91	—	6.88	—	5.91	—
2	8.10	—	7.56	—	6.65	—
3	8.38	7.68	7.62	7.60	7.08	5.65
4	9.28	8.83	9.00	8.02	7.55	6.01
5	9.59	9.52	8.82	8.76	7.90	6.29
6	10.32	10.23	9.82	9.04	8.57	6.91
7	11.14	10.83	9.75	8.94	9.01	7.52
8	11.59	11.24	10.71	10.37	9.52	9.49
9	11.79	11.09	10.96	10.05	9.26	8.78
10	12.34	12.59	10.68	11.79	9.41	11.03
11	13.00	11.82	11.17	10.69	10.18	11.21
12	12.84	14.06	11.70	13.27	10.65	11.24

The most prominent feature, however, is that the oral and written averages are similar for any given group in any given year. In other words, in reference to average number of words per communication unit, the subjects tend to speak *and* write in units of virtually the same average length.

Special Study of Dependent Clauses

Whenever teachers discuss syntactic growth, they encounter disagreement concerning the significance of dependent clauses. Certainly it is true that sentence complexity is not necessarily a virtue; multiple embeddings can obfuscate rather than illuminate meanings. On the other hand, research has established by now the fact that elaboration and complexity of syntax are clearly measures of development in oral and written language.

Disagreement on this matter could be resolved by an awareness that both sides of the question have validity, that the resolution of the disagreement lies in a reconciliation of opposing views. During his lifetime, Francis Christensen took the position that dependent clauses are often a sign of bad style; he objected to the research of Kellogg Hunt and John Mellon, who showed dependent clauses tallying with more mature writing. The resolution of this controversy is persuasively stated by James Moffett.[7] He agrees that complicated sentences can make for awful writing, but he also believes the dynamics of language growth clearly indicate that "children's sentences must grow rank before they can be trimmed." He sees the need for children to discover, through speaking and writing, the syntactical strategies "that answer the felt needs of their maturing thought, their exchanges in conversation, and their efforts to fit what they write to what they have to say. There is good reason to believe that the final answer to linguistic elaboration lies beyond language, in general cognitive development, and that intellectual stimulation is far more likely to accelerate syntactic growth than grammar knowledge."

In this research, we have, among other approaches, compared the three groups on the basis of their dependent clauses. Such clauses are obviously an important element in elaborated usage.

Average Number of Dependent Clauses per Communication Unit—Oral Language

For oral language the data on average number of dependent clauses per communication unit indicate among the groups an even more striking disparity than found on previous measures. (See Table 8 and Figure 5.) If one examines the relative growth calculations, it can be seen that the High group reaches the 63% level in grade four, whereas the Low group does not achieve this level until grade eleven.[8] One interesting phenomenon is the spurt of growth exhibited by the Low group in grade twelve; even so, at the *conclusion* of high school the Low group tends to be approximately five years behind the High group. Again, the Random subject falls between the High and Low groups, generally several years ahead of the Low group and several years behind the High group.

Another interesting facet of the data is that the Low group moves from 20% at grade one to 79% at grade twelve, representing a *four-fold increase*, whereas the High group's movement from 41% to 115% indicates only a *three-fold increase*. The Low group does in fact exhibit substantial growth—a growth which, purely in percentage terms, is rather striking. Thus one may hypothesize that the Low group's fundamental problem with syntax may arise from low socioeconomic status and a different early language environment.

Table 8

Average Number of Dependent Clauses Per Communication Unit—Oral Language

	Average Number of Dependent Clauses per Unit (mean)			Relative Growth[a] (in percent)			Year-to-Year Velocity[b] (in percent)		
Grade	High Group	Random Group	Low Group	High Group	Random Group	Low Group	High Group	Random Group	Low Group
1	0.24	0.16	0.12	41.38	27.59	20.69	—	—	—
2	0.25	0.21	0.17	43.10	36.21	29.31	+ 1.72	+ 8.62	+ 8.62
3	0.27	0.22	0.18	46.55	37.93	31.03	+ 3.45	+ 1.72	+ 1.72
4	0.37	0.30	0.20	63.79	51.72	34.48	+17.24	+13.79	+ 3.45
5	0.37	0.29	0.25	63.79	50.00	43.10	0.00	- 1.72	+ 8.62
6	0.41	0.37	0.30	70.69	63.79	51.72	+ 6.90	+13.79	+ 8.62
7	0.44	0.35	0.31	75.86	60.34	53.45	+ 5.17	- 3.45	+ 1.73
8	0.45	0.39	0.30	77.59	67.24	51.72	+ 1.73	+ 6.90	- 1.73
9	0.52	0.43	0.31	89.66	74.14	53.45	+12.07	+ 6.90	+ 1.73
10	0.61	0.48	0.33	105.17	82.76	56.90	-15.51	+ 8.62	+ 3.45
11	0.63	0.52	0.36	108.62	89.66	62.07	+ 3.45	+ 6.90	+ 5.17
12	0.67	0.58	0.46	115.52	100.00	79.31	+ 6.90	+10.34	+17.24

[a]Relative Growth uses the Random group at grade twelve to equal 100 percent.
[b]Year-to-Year Velocity is the percentage change in any given group from one year to the following year.

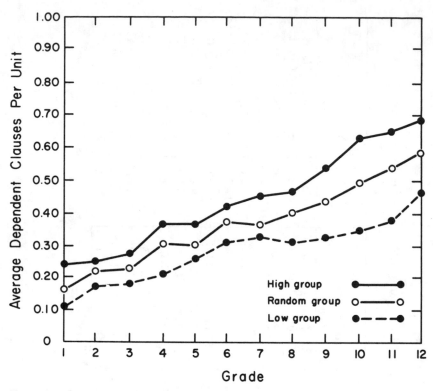

Fig. 5. Average number of dependent clauses per communication unit—oral language (mean).

Average Number of Dependent Clauses per Communication Unit—Written Language

In written language the data on average number of dependent clauses per communication unit for all three groups are considerably more alike after elementary school than any of the measures presented previously. (See Table 9 and Figure 6.) In grades four through eight the High group evidences an obvious superiority over both the Low and Random groups. But in grade nine the pattern grows less clear; and in grades ten and eleven, the Low group, despite beginning at a low level, has rapidly forged ahead and for one year catches up to the High and Random groups.

However, when one reads the actual compositions, the *quality* of writing produced by the Low group is obviously weak in comparison to that of the High or Random groups—not only because of poor spelling, punctuation, and usage but more especially because of a general lack of coherence and organization of content.[9] Also, superior writers often prefer a tighter way to coil their thoughts than dependent clauses permit. For example:

Dependent Clause: After he had finished the crossword puzzle, he went to bed.

Tighter: Having finished the crossword puzzle, he went to bed.

Thus, to reach a valid conclusion one must look beyond the statistical data on dependent clauses.

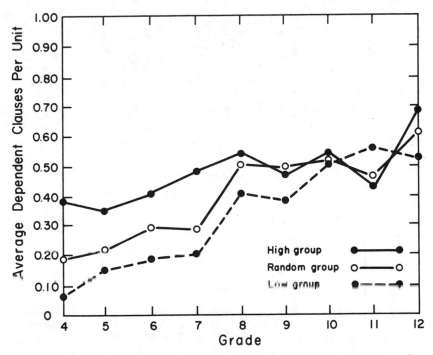

Fig. 6. Average number of dependent clauses per communication unit—written language (mean).

Words in Dependent Clauses as a Percentage of Words in Communication Units—Oral Language

One further method of examining the dependent clause is to calculate the number of words used in dependent clauses as a percentage of the number of words used in communication units. In this way it is possible to ascertain the growth of the dependent clause portion of the unit (parallel to our method of determining the growth in the overall length of the unit).[10]

The first obvious feature of the data is that each group exhibits a steady upward trend, indicating that with increasing chronological

Table 9

Average Number of Dependent Clauses per Communication Unit—Written Language

Grade	Average Number of Dependent Clauses per Communication Unit (mean)			Relative Growth[a] (in percent)			Year-to-Year Velocity[b] (in percent)		
	High Group	Random Group	Low Group	High Group	Random Group	Low Group	High Group	Random Group	Low Group
4	0.38	0.19	0.06	63.33	31.67	10.00	—	—	—
5	0.35	0.21	0.14	58.33	35.00	23.33	− 5.00	+ 3.33	+13.33
6	0.40	0.29	0.18	66.67	48.33	30.00	+ 8.32	+13.33	+ 6.67
7	0.48	0.28	0.20	80.00	46.67	33.33	+13.33	− 1.66	+ 3.33
8	0.54	0.50	0.40	90.00	83.33	66.67	+10.00	+36.66	+33.34
9	0.46	0.47	0.37	76.67	78.33	61.67	−13.33	− 5.00	− 5.00
10	0.53	0.52	0.51	88.33	86.67	85.00	+11.66	+ 8.34	+23.33
11	0.43	0.45	0.55	71.67	75.00	91.67	−16.66	−11.67	+ 6.67
12	0.66	0.60	0.52	110.00	100.00	86.67	+38.33	+25.00	− 5.00

[a]Relative Growth uses the Random group at grade twelve to equal 100 percent.
[b]Year-to-Year Velocity is the percentage change in any given group from one year to the following year.

age all subjects devote an increasing proportion of their spoken language to the dependent clause portion of their communication units. (See Table 10 and Figure 7.) As the reader will note, between grades one and eight the subjects go through several stages which may be considered pauses or consolidations before achieving further growth.

Also of considerable interest is the fact that the High group exhibits approximately the same degree of superiority on this oral measure as it has on average number of words per total communication unit, remaining approximately four years above the Low group and two years above the Random group. In addition, the lines on the graph never cross, and there exists about the same degree of difference among the groups at grade twelve as at grade one.

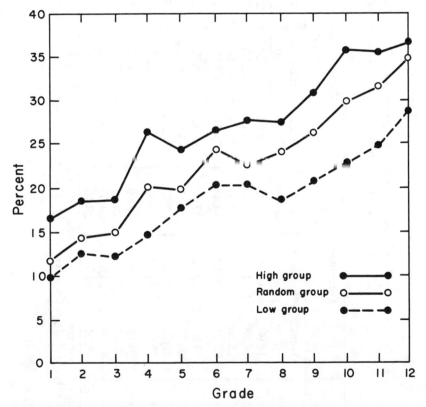

Fig. 7. Words in dependent clauses as a percentage of words in communication units—oral language.

Table 10

Words in Dependent Clauses as a Percentage of Words in Communication Units—Oral Language

Grade	Percentage			Relative Growth[a] (in percent)			Year-to-Year Velocity[b] (in percent)		
	High Group	Random Group	Low Group	High Group	Random Group	Low Group	High Group	Random Group	Low Group
1	16.60	11.82	9.42	48.03	34.20	27.26	—	—	—
2	18.38	14.64	12.14	53.18	42.36	35.13	+ 5.15	+ 8.16	+ 7.87
3	18.50	14.86	12.07	53.53	43.00	34.92	+ 0.35	+ 0.64	- 0.21
4	26.21	20.07	14.46	75.84	58.07	41.84	+22.31	+15.07	+ 6.92
5	23.98	19.62	17.53	69.39	56.77	50.72	- 6.45	- 1.30	+ 8.88
6	26.22	24.28	20.16	75.87	70.25	58.33	+ 6.48	+13.48	+ 7.61
7	27.73	22.22	20.20	80.24	64.29	58.45	+ 4.37	- 5.96	+ 0.12
8	26.94	23.34	18.52	77.95	67.53	53.59	- 2.29	+ 3.24	- 4.86
9	30.14	25.80	20.56	87.21	74.65	59.49	+ 9.26	+ 7.12	+ 5.90
10	35.64	29.69	22.26	103.12	85.91	64.41	+15.91	+11.26	+ 4.92
11	35.49	30.93	24.05	102.69	89.50	69.59	- 0.43	+ 3.59	+ 5.18
12	36.34	34.56	28.78	105.15	100.00	83.28	+ 2.46	+10.50	+13.69

[a]Relative Growth uses the Random group at grade twelve to equal 100 percent.
[b]Year-to-Year Velocity is the percentage change in any given group from one year to the following year.

Words in Dependent Clauses as a Percentage of Words in Communication Units—Written Language

In written language the data on words in dependent clauses as a percentage of words in communication units contain the same peculiarities the investigator indicated previously in reference to the average number of written dependent clauses per unit. The data seem to discriminate clearly among the groups *until* grade nine, but following that year there is a criss-cross phenomenon on the graphs and an obvious catching-up process by the Low group. (See Table 11 and Figure 8.)

However, an examination of the written protocols shows the *quality* of the High group's compositions to be notably superior to that of the Low group in grades eight through twelve. Therefore,

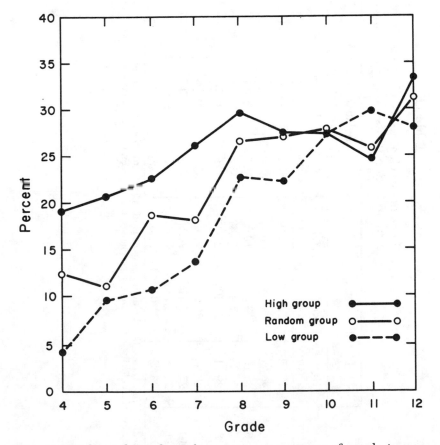

Fig. 8. Words in dependent clauses as a percentage of words in communication units—written language.

Table 11

Words in Dependent Clauses as a Percentage of Words in Communication Units—Written Language

Grade	Percentage			Relative Growth[a] (in percent)			Year-to-Year Velocity[b] (in percent)		
	High Group	Random Group	Low Group	High Group	Random Group	Low Group	High Group	Random Group	Low Group
4	19.02	12.68	4.04	61.26	40.84	13.01	—	—	—
5	20.38	11.02	9.40	65.64	35.49	30.27	+ 4.38	− 5.35	+17.26
6	22.16	18.55	10.63	71.37	59.74	34.24	+ 5.73	+24.25	+ 3.97
7	26.03	17.95	13.47	83.83	57.81	43.38	+12.46	− 1.93	+ 9.14
8	29.71	26.30	22.38	95.68	84.70	72.08	+11.85	+26.89	+28.70
9	26.86	26.67	21.62	86.51	85.89	69.63	− 9.17	+ 1.19	− 2.45
10	27.04	27.47	27.16	87.09	88.47	87.47	+ 0.58	+ 2.58	+17.84
11	24.38	25.28	29.37	78.52	81.42	94.59	− 8.57	− 7.05	+ 7.12
12	33.82	31.05	27.58	108.92	100.00	88.82	+30.40	+18.58	− 5.77

[a]Relative Growth uses the Random group at grade twelve to equal 100 percent.
[b]Year-to-Year Velocity is the percentage change in any given group from one year to the following year.

despite the statistical data, which deals only with the dependent clause and not all important features of written syntax and language strategy, we can *not* conclude that the Low group has caught up to the High group. What, then, is happening? The explanation is that dependent clauses are not the only or necessarily always the best syntactic strategy for subordinating elements of thought. More sophisticated strategies include the following: appositives; nominative absolutes; noun, verb, and adjective clusters in cumulative sentences; gerunds, participles, and infinitives— simple or expanded. The Low group uses dependent clauses excessively in high school.

The mathematics underlying Figure 8, therefore, are based upon a count in which the more mature syntactical strategies are not included. Thus, the sequence of events for written language is that in grades eight through twelve the High group uses a more sophisticated style *in lieu of* dependent clauses, making it appear as if the Low group is closing the earlier gap between the groups—as indeed it is, so far as dependent clauses are concerned. Later in this monograph data will be presented on a weighted index of elaboration which includes other structures as well as dependent clauses; for *this* measure of written language, the High group demonstrates a consistent superiority over the Random and Low groups.

Proportion of Noun, Adjectival, and Adverbial Clauses—Oral Language

To determine whether or not the groups exhibit any shift in the kinds of dependent clauses they use, each dependent clause was categorized as noun, adjective, or adverb; their incidence was then tallied and converted to a percentage to show the proportions of noun, adjectival, and adverbial clauses actually used by the High, Low, and Random groups. (See Table 12 and Figure 9. Figure 9 shows data on Random group only; the Random group, typical of the subjects as a whole, should be of most use to curriculum makers.) Of the three kinds of clauses, adjectival clauses are the most interesting. Whether or not the adjectival clause is a *later* development in language than the use of either noun or adverbial clauses has been discussed by other researchers.[11]

For oral language, our findings on proportions of dependent clauses show the adjectival clause to be an important development for the High group (rising from approximately 22% in the early years to 33% in the later years). In the Low and Random groups,

Table 12

Proportion of Noun, Adjectival, and Adverbial Clauses—Oral Language (in percent)[a]

Grade	Noun Clauses			Adjectival Clauses			Adverbial Clauses		
	High Group	*Random Group*	*Low Group*	*High Group*	*Random Group*	*Low Group*	*High Group*	*Random Group*	*Low Group*
1	45.84	41.48	33.56	23.23	26.18	19.09	30.93	32.34	47.35
2	54.91	44.75	35.07	20.50	25.21	18.86	24.59	30.04	46.07
3	53.40	43.05	46.79	22.65	27.83	21.55	23.95	29.12	31.66
4	45.15	49.63	50.35	20.84	19.90	21.41	34.01	30.47	28.24
5	45.74	48.19	51.72	26.90	21.91	19.98	27.36	29.90	28.30
6	47.38	47.06	52.06	22.53	21.10	22.36	30.09	31.84	25.58
7	38.98	41.12	53.02	30.03	30.15	21.27	30.99	28.73	25.71
8	36.52	37.14	29.79	35.30	34.24	31.05	28.18	28.62	39.16
9	37.11	43.70	49.32	38.30	30.85	21.37	24.59	25.45	29.31
10	43.35	44.54	47.74	30.20	25.50	20.43	26.45	29.96	31.83
11	40.66	46.67	44.67	33.76	24.06	27.00	25.58	29.27	28.33
12	43.34	50.27	45.25	33.05	24.69	20.73	23.61	25.04	34.02

[a]Noun + adjectival + adverbial add up to 100.00 percent in all cases (on a year-by-year basis for each group).

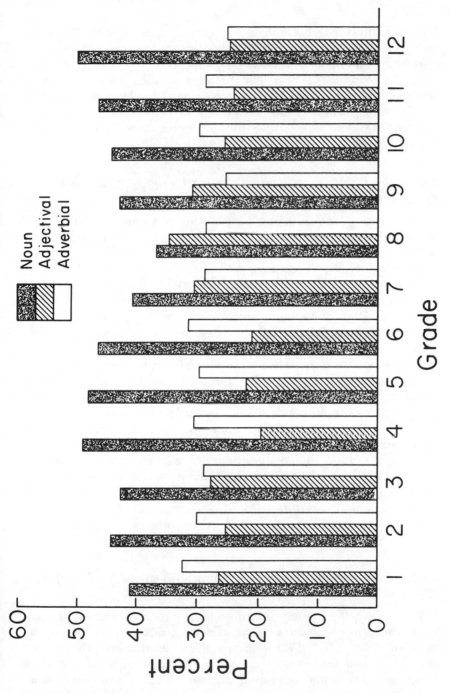

Fig. 9. Proportion of noun, adjectival, and adverbial clauses—Random group, oral language.

however, the subjects show some yearly fluctuations on this measure, but at the end of the high school years they use virtually the identical percentage of adjectival clauses they used in grade one. Thus the evidence seems clear that an exceptional speaker (High) will use a progressively greater percentage of adjectival clauses in oral language, whereas the nonproficient speaker (Low) or average speaker (Random) will show no such percentage increase in the use of adjectival clauses.

Proportion of Noun, Adjectival and Adverbial Clauses—Written Language

For written language, the proportions of noun, adjectival, and adverbial clauses are less well defined than for oral language (see Table 13). In the case of written adjectival clauses, all groups tend to use an increasing proportion from grades five through twelve, although the notable feature is that the *Low* group in grades eleven and twelve uses a higher percentage of adjectival clauses than either the High or Random group. Once again we note the High group's dexterity in subordination strategy, replacing dependent clauses with a repertoire of more effective word clusters.

It is important to note here that Hunt's careful research on children's writing shows the adjective dependent clause increasing steadily from the earliest grades to the latest, and among skilled adult writers the adjective clause is still more frequent than it is with students finishing high school. In our own research, we are especially interested in the fact that the High group excels in incidence of written adjectival dependent clauses until grade ten. At that point the Low group begins to manifest what the High group has exemplified throughout the early grades, and the High group, if one inspects its written compositions, transfers its emphases to adjectival participial phrases and other more sophisticated solutions.

Relative Growth and Velocity of Noun, Adjectival, and Adverbial Clauses—Oral Language

In Table 8 the average number of dependent clauses per oral communication unit shows a substantial *growth* in the use of dependent clauses by all three groups. The *relative growth rates* on this date (as distinguished from velocity) have been calculated for noun, adjectival, and adverbial clauses, as have the year-to-year velocities on these same data. (See Tables 14 and 15 and Figures 10, 11, and 12.)[12]

Table 13

Proportion of Noun, Adjectival, and Adverbial Clauses—Written Language (in percent)[a]

Grade	Noun Clauses			Adjectival Clauses			Adverbial Clauses		
	High Group	Random Group	Low Group	High Group	Random Group	Low Group	High Group	Random Group	Low Group
4	37.32	40.78	38.33	31.45	25.79	46.67	31.23	33.43	15.00
5	24.93	28.69	42.81	25.22	14.26	19.28	49.86	57.05	37.91
6	34.37	44.60	39.06	15.86	16.32	35.42	49.77	39.08	25.52
7	27.68	26.63	38.12	23.65	18.77	12.80	48.67	54.60	49.08
8	37.47	37.39	31.16	26.13	21.60	23.70	36.40	41.00	45.14
9	37.04	32.40	37.57	20.49	27.89	24.56	42.47	39.70	37.87
10	34.59	31.15	32.21	30.91	34.22	27.91	34.50	34.63	39.88
11	36.40	33.95	35.06	31.86	39.19	40.14	31.74	26.86	24.80
12	33.71	29.58	29.65	31.46	33.91	37.75	34.83	36.51	32.60

[a]Noun + adjectival + adverbial add up to 100.00 percent in all cases (on a year-by-year basis for each group).

Table 14

Relative Growth Rate of Noun, Adjectival, and Adverbial Clauses—Oral Language
(in percent)[a]

Grade	Noun Clauses			Adjectival Clauses			Adverbial Clauses			Total Dependent Clauses		
	High Group	Random Group	Low Group	High Group	Random Group	Low Group	High Group	Random Group	Low Group	High Group	Random Group	Low Group
1	38.34	26.42	18.18	35.69	27.66	13.73	50.70	30.77	33.59	40.73	27.76	20.86
2	47.03	35.11	24.44	38.92	38.92	27.45	43.45	39.93	44.37	44.10	37.20	30.12
3	49.70	34.41	26.76	44.41	42.35	25.39	46.27	44.86	43.66	47.52	38.99	30.64
4	62.57	53.88	32.67	51.68	44.41	30.20	77.68	57.25	45.56	63.57	52.32	35.29
5	61.87	48.77	45.29	66.58	46.47	32.05	67.11	59.15	49.08	64.37	50.76	42.88
6	67.19	61.52	54.57	65.41	59.51	40.49	85.21	74.44	56.34	71.22	64.26	51.50
7	57.59	45.99	54.92	90.12	73.92	45.78	99.30	76.55	60.35	76.13	60.61	53.94
8	53.98	49.01	34.41	110.50	97.46	64.04	93.87	77.25	77.25	78.17	68.19	52.49
9	65.94	62.56	47.62	135.90	102.06	48.25	95.28	71.83	70.42	90.91	74.80	53.49
10	90.72	73.44	52.59	125.60	83.05	48.25	114.08	105.42	74.44	105.28	83.78	56.96
11	90.37	84.12	56.90	146.40	90.12	67.26	113.38	100.70	70.42	110.26	89.74	62.92
12	97.32	100.00	76.47	154.22	100.00	65.41	118.10	100.00	101.20	116.86	100.00	79.78

[a]Using the Random group at grade twelve to equal 100 percent.

Table 15

Year-to-Year Velocity of Relative Growth Rates for Noun, Adjectival, and Adverbial Clauses—Oral Language
(in percent)

Grade	High Group			Random Group			Low Group		
	Noun	Adjectival	Adverbial	Noun	Adjectival	Adverbial	Noun	Adjectival	Adverbial
1	—	—	—	—	—	—	—	—	—
2	+ 8.69	+ 3.23	− 7.25	− 8.69	+11.26	+ 9.16	+ 6.26	+13.72	+10.78
3	+ 2.67	+ 5.49	+ 2.82	− 0.70	+ 3.43	+ 4.93	+ 2.32	− 2.06	− 0.71
4	+12.87	+ 7.27	+31.41	+19.47	+ 2.06	+12.39	+ 5.91	+ 4.81	+ 1.90
5	− 0.70	+14.90	−10.57	− 5.11	+ 2.06	+ 1.90	+12.62	+ 1.85	+ 3.52
6	+ 5.32	− 1.17	+18.10	+12.75	+13.04	+15.29	+ 9.28	+ 8.44	+ 7.26
7	− 9.60	+24.71	+14.09	−15.53	+14.41	+ 2.11	+ 0.35	+ 5.29	+ 4.01
8	− 3.61	+20.38	− 5.43	+ 3.02	+23.54	+ 0.70	−20.51	+18.26	+16.90
9	+11.96	+25.40	+ 1.41	+13.55	+ 4.60	− 5.42	+13.21	−15.79	− 6.83
10	+24.78	−10.30	+18.80	+10.88	−19.01	+33.59	+ 4.97	0.00	+ 4.02
11	− 0.35	+20.80	− 0.70	+10.68	+ 7.07	− 4.72	+ 4.31	+19.01	− 4.02
12	+ 6.95	+ 7.82	+ 4.72	+15.88	+ 9.88	− 0.70	+19.57	− 1.85	+30.78
Twelve-Year Growth Total[a]	+58.98	+118.53	+67.40	+73.58	+72.34	+69.23	+58.29	+51.68	+67.61

[a]Calculated directly from Table 14—Grade Twelve minus Grade One = Twelve-Year Growth Total.

High Group   97.32 − 38.34 = 58.98 (noun)
           154.22 − 35.69 = 118.53 (adjectival)
           118.10 − 50.70 = 67.40 (adverbial)

Random Group   100.00 − 26.42 = 73.58 (noun)
           100.00 − 27.66 = 72.34 (adjectival)
           100.00 − 30.77 = 69.23 (adverbial)

Low Group   76.47 − 18.18 = 58.29 (noun)
           65.41 − 13.73 = 51.68 (adjectival)
           101.20 − 33.59 = 67.61 (adverbial)

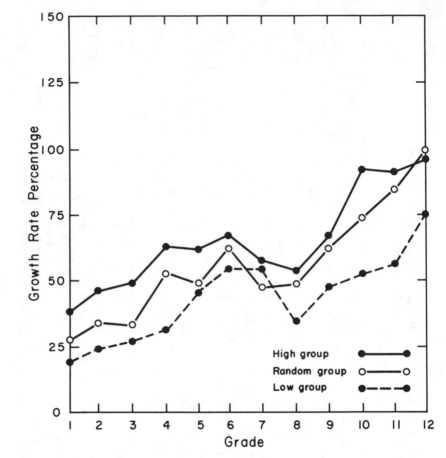

Fig. 10. Relative growth rate of noun clauses—oral language; Random group at grade twelve equals 100 percent.

In examining the *growth* data, the most striking feature is the High group's huge growth in using *adjectival* clauses orally (35% in grade one to 154% in grade twelve).

Stages of growth are seen most clearly in the year-to-year velocities calculated for each group (see Table 15). This computation is simply a *subtraction* showing the *difference* between the growth rates of any group from one year to the next. For example, the High group's noun clauses for grade two (47.03) minus grade one (38.34) equals 8.69, which is the velocity between grades one and two. From this calculation, one can see that the High group's growth in adjectival clauses is centered mainly in junior high school, grades 7, 8, and 9. The reader is invited to make other visual comparisons of the velocity figures, such as grade eight, a

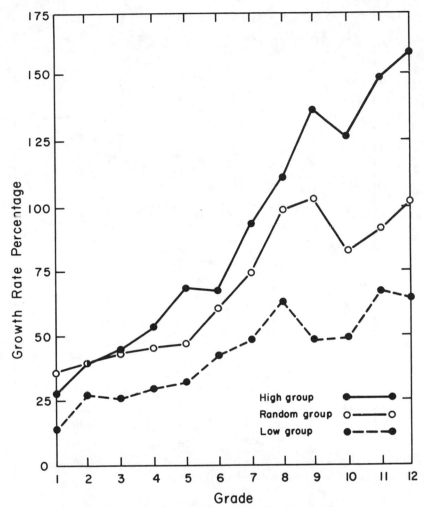

Fig. 11. Relative growth rate of adjectival clauses—oral language; Random group at grade twelve equals 100 percent.

year in which *all* groups show a large increase in the use of *adjective* clauses, or grade twelve, the year of the Low group's large increase in *adverbial* clauses.

Functions of Noun Clauses—Oral Language

In previous data on the use of dependent clauses, the High group showed an obvious superiority over both the Random and Low groups, indicating that in oral language the High group's development is approximately two years above the Random group and four to five years above the Low group.

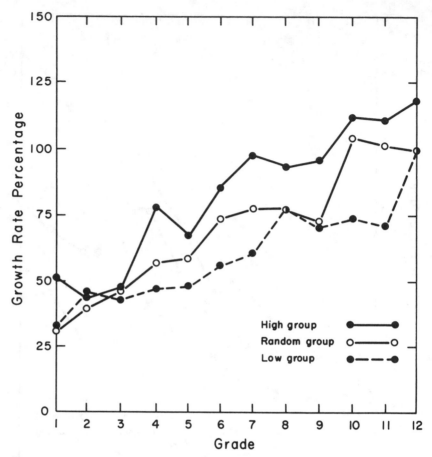

Fig. 12. Relative growth rate of adverbial clauses—oral language; Random group at grade twelve equals 100 percent.

In the present analysis our purpose is to focus on the *functions of noun clauses*, keeping total noun clauses per group per year equal to 100% in order to discover whether or not any group exhibits substantial *shifts* in frequency of use of the various functions of noun clauses. (For example, at grade five, the High group uses noun clauses in these proportions: 69.52% as direct object, 19.25% as predicate nominative, 11.23% in other uses, or 100% altogether.) We are asking these questions:

1. With increasing chronological age, does the High group use a greater proportion of noun clauses as subjects or appositives than either the Low or Random group? Subjects and appositives would seem to represent more unusual strategies of syntax.

2. Does the Low group concentrate almost exclusively on the simple and easy use of noun clauses as direct objects, thus showing, as Lawton found, a *more restricted repertoire* of noun clause functions than either the High or Random group?

3. Are there obvious differences, with the High group at one extreme, the Low group at the opposite extreme, and the Random group in the center?

The most obvious feature of the data is that, *in oral language, all groups* tend to concentrate their usage of noun clauses in either direct objects or predicate nominatives. However, if one examines all other types of noun clauses, it becomes clear that an increase in chronological age does in fact cause all three groups to shift some usage to the less common categories of noun clauses, with pronounced surges in this direction occurring at grades seven, nine, and eleven. No one uses noun clauses very often as subjects or appositives, but in writing the High group does use these more frequently than the Low group.

A less apparent feature of the data—although undoubtedly the most important—is that when one examines the other categories of noun clauses, no group exhibits any remarkable shifts or trends clearly distinguishing it from any other group. If one were to graph the various pieces of data, one would notice similar upward trends for *all* groups in categories such as object of preposition or object of infinitive. Only the Low group demonstrates a fairly consistent superiority in the use of noun clauses as direct objects, an easy, common, and early function identified by Lawton.

Functions of Noun Clauses—Written Language

The analysis of noun clauses in the subjects' written language is identical in all respects to that of oral language. In many respects the conclusions are virtually identical, except that for *all* groups the upward spurt in the use of all other noun clauses occurs at grade eight in written language rather than at grade seven as in oral language. Our research, both in oral and in written language, tallies with the research of Lawton in Great Britain. Lawton, using writing for his evidence, found noun clauses used as objects very common and learned early in life, but noun clauses used as nominals—as subjects and appositives—were later and less frequent developments.[13]

In writing, the High and Random groups use a greater proportion of the less common functions of the noun clause than does the Low group. This difference indicates a tendency for the High and

Random groups to use a greater proportion of noun clauses as appositives, objects of prepositions, objects of adjectives, and objects of participles than does the Low group. Altogether, the findings appear largely uncertain rather than indicating positive differences. The research of Hunt, the Peabody Group, and Bateman and Zidonis should be read for further evidence on written language.[14]

Types of Adverbial Clauses—Oral Language

Adverbial clauses have been analyzed in the same manner as noun clauses; keeping total adverbial clauses per group per year equal to 100% facilitates detection of any substantial shifts in their use. *Time* and *cause* are the two types of adverbial clauses used most frequently by every group, accounting for approximately 75% of all adverbial clauses. However, when looking at all other functions of adverbial clauses, we find a different trend than we found for noun clauses. With adverbial clauses there is no specific grade in which the percent figures indicate a sudden upward surge. Instead, the percentages are relatively stable; approximately the same proportions appear in the early years as in the later years, with only grades eleven and twelve showing marked upward movement. However, the percentages for the High group tend to be higher in the less-common adverbial clauses of consequence and concession.[15]

Types of Adverbial Clauses—Written Language

Adverbial clauses in written language were analyzed in the same manner as those in oral language, with total adverbial clauses of all types per group per year equalling 100%. Again, as in oral language, the predominant type of adverbial clauses in written language are clauses of *time* and *cause*. However, the use of all other types of adverbial clauses fluctuated much more erratically than in oral language. If the nature of the composition topic is such that time and cause are dominant features, this characteristic in turn precipitates high percentages in those categories, whereas if the nature of the composition topic is more reflective, one can expect higher percentages in other categories. This corresponds to the findings of Hunt who reports: "Movable adverb clauses do seem to increase with maturity in the very early grades, but the ceiling is reached early, and after the middle grades the frequency of them tells more about the mode of discourse and subject matter than about maturity."[16]

Other than clauses of *time* or *cause*, adverbial clauses of *condition* are those most commonly used by all groups in speech and writing. Over the period of grades four through twelve the High group does employ more clauses of *concession*, both in speech and writing. There are no obvious differences with respect to clauses of *purpose, manner,* and *place*.

We were interested in all these matters of dependent clauses because LaBrant's research on written language showed the number of dependent clauses increased with students' age, as did complexity and clarity of thought.[17] LaBrant also found the least-used dependent clauses to be noun clauses and adverbial clauses of condition, concession, place, purpose, result, and comparison, all constituting at each mental age less than 6% of the total clauses written. Wherein do the results of this research agree or disagree with LaBrant? Noun clauses used as subjects or appositives prove to be rare, but used as objects and predicate nominatives, they are frequently employed by all subjects. Adverbial clauses of *consequence* and *concession* are used more frequently by the High group in speaking, and in writing this group uses clauses of *concession* more frequently. In adverbial clauses of concession, the meaning or thought is in some way opposed to the main statement but not in contradiction to it; usually the dependent adverbial clause of concession begins with *though* or *although*. Logically this appears be a complicated balancing of relationships and may accompany superior ability to put thoughts into words.

We conclude that the topic of any writing or speaking shifts the frequency of dependent clause functions. However, clauses requiring rigorous attention to relationships will appear less frequently in all language and will be employed more often by those who are skilled in expression.

Index of Elaboration

In this research, elaboration is the use of *all strategies* by which communication units are expanded beyond simple one-word subjects and predicates. We are interested in modification and coordination, not only through dependent clauses but also through adjectives, adverbs, prepositional phrases, infinitives, appositives, gerunds, and all other means of expansion.

Elaboration Index—Oral Language

For all three groups, the average number of spoken elaboration points per communication unit moves steadily upward. In the

Random and Low groups, grades eight through ten, we find plateaus indicating consolidation phases before further growth. (See Table 16 and Figure 13.) Just as on other language measures, the High group is approximately four years in advance of the Low group and two years ahead of the Random group. For example, the High group achieves 53% of its growth by grade one whereas the Low group arrives at the fifth grade before such an achievement.

What is of the greatest significance, however, is the evidence that this elaboration index for oral language reveals almost identical results as the measure of average number of words per communication unit and does so for all three groups. The reader should compare Figure 1 with Figure 13; the graphs for the two measures are almost identical. One of our analysts, reflecting on the amount of time she had spent tallying elaboration units, reflected on whether or not the additional elaboration analysis had been justified. We very much believe that it was justified, for now we feel secure in using the simpler and easier count of average number of words per communication unit. Schools wishing to ascertain language growth can by-pass the time-consuming elaboration analysis, and many aspects of research can rely upon the simpler count, now that we have validated it. To be sure there will be other times when the analysis of elaboration will be desired, but for most purposes the simpler count will be all that is necessary.[18]

In year-to-year velocity of growth, the High group exhibited a strong upward shift in grades six and seven; *all* groups demonstrated such a shift in grade eleven. Another interesting way to examine the data is to view each group individually, noting that large upward shifts are typically followed by either retrenchment or a substantially lessened amount of growth in a subsequent year (see Figure 13). This is especially true of the Random group.

Elaboration Index—Written Language

For written language the average number of elaboration points per communication unit indicates that the High group demonstrates the same degree of superiority over the Low and Random groups as in oral language. They remain approximately four years above the Low group and two years above the Random group. For example, the High group's average of 4.12 in grade four is not exceeded by the Low group until grade eight; more importantly, the superiority of the High group is *consistent* from grade four through grade twelve. (See Table 17 and Figure 14.)

Here we would like to stress that this superiority of the High group is particularly worthy of note because this consistency was

Table 16

Average Number of Elaboration Index Points Per Communication Unit—Oral Language

Grade	Elaboration Points per Unit			Relative Growth[a]			Year-to-Year Velocity[b]		
	High Group	Random Group	Low Group	High Group	Random Group	Low Group	High Group	Random Group	Low Group
1	3.18	2.47	2.05	52.56	40.83	33.88	—	—	—
2	3.05	2.73	2.43	50.41	45.12	40.17	− 2.15	+ 4.29	+ 6.29
3	3.33	2.78	2.57	55.04	45.95	42.48	+ 4.63	+ 0.83	+ 2.31
4	3.96	3.63	2.98	65.45	60.00	49.26	+10.41	+14.05	+ 6.78
5	4.14	3.67	3.12	68.43	60.66	51.57	+ 2.98	+ 0.66	+ 2.31
6	4.77	4.33	3.46	78.84	71.57	57.19	+10.41	+10.91	+ 5.62
7	5.36	4.38	3.94	88.60	72.40	65.12	+ 9.76	+ 0.83	+ 7.93
8	5.48	4.95	4.24	90.58	81.82	70.08	+ 1.98	+ 9.42	+ 4.96
9	5.70	5.16	4.16	94.21	85.29	68.76	+ 3.63	+ 3.47	− 1.32
10	5.93	5.11	4.22	98.02	84.46	69.75	+ 3.81	− 0.83	+ 0.99
11	6.80	5.75	4.92	112.40	95.04	81.32	+14.38	+10.58	+11.57
12	6.92	6.05	5.41	114.38	100.00	89.42	+ 1.98	+ 4.96	+ 8.10

[a]Relative Growth uses the Random group at grade twelve to equal 100 percent.
[b]Year-to-Year Velocity is the percentage change in any given group from one year to the following year.

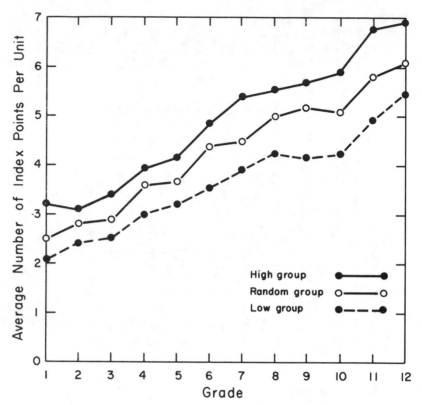

Fig. 13. Weighted index of elaboration—oral language.

not found when we examined *only* dependent clauses in the subjects' writing. In other words, the elaboration index indicates that *the High group shows an obvious superiority when ALL elaborated structures are considered* whereas such a superiority does not exist (on written language during the high school years) if one ignores other elaborated structures and concentrates exclusively on dependent clauses.

The greatest velocity of growth for the High group occurs in grades six, seven, and eleven. Velocity for the Random group is particularly interesting since this group represents all the population in the schools. The Random group made notable advances in grades five, eight, ten, and twelve. These surges in writing occur one or two years subsequent to similar surges on oral language elaboration. All three groups slow up or fall back in grade nine.

Table 17

Average Number of Elaboration Index Points Per Communication Unit—Written Language

Grade	Elaboration Points per Unit			Relative Growth[a]			Year-to-Year Velocity[b]		
	High Group	Random Group	Low Group	High Group	Random Group	Low Group	High Group	Random Group	Low Group
4	4.12	3.29	2.73	52.55	41.96	34.82	—	—	—
5	4.51	4.08	2.64	57.53	52.04	33.67	+ 4.98	+10.08	− 1.15
6	5.06	4.18	3.12	64.54	53.32	39.80	+ 7.01	+ 1.28	+ 6.13
7	5.62	4.07	3.36	71.68	51.91	42.86	+ 7.14	− 1.41	+ 3.06
8	6.22	6.05	4.89	79.34	77.17	62.37	+ 7.66	+25.26	+19.51
9	6.41	5.25	4.33	81.76	66.96	55.23	+ 2.42	−10.21	− 7.14
10	7.15	6.79	5.40	91.20	86.61	68.88	+ 9.44	+19.65	+13.65
11	6.38	5.97	5.72	81.38	76.15	72.96	− 9.82	−10.46	+ 4.08
12	8.51	7.84	6.11	108.55	100.00	77.93	+27.17	+23.85	+ 4.97

[a]Relative Growth uses the Random group at grade twelve to equal 100 percent.
[b]Year-to-Year Velocity is the percentage change in any given group from one year to the following year.

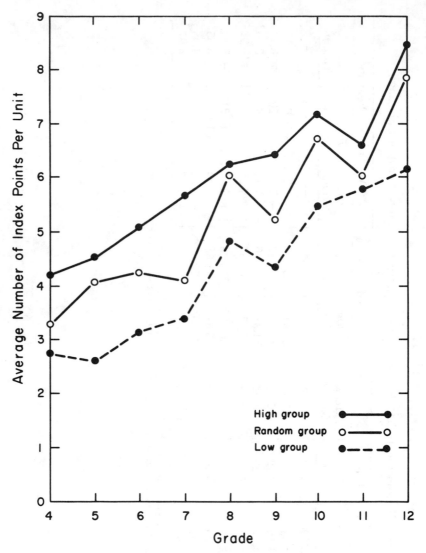

Fig. 14. Weighted index of elaboration—written language.

Comparison of Oral and Written Language

Several interesting facets of the data may be observed by placing the oral and written elaboration averages side-by-side (see Table 18). First, the High group, with the exception of grade eleven, demonstrates a consistently higher number of elaboration points on written language than on oral language. This slowly becomes the pattern for the Random group, also. Apparently less

Table 18

Average Number of Elaboration Points Per Communication Unit

	High Group		Random Group		Low Group	
Grade	Oral	Written	Oral	Written	Oral	Written
1	3.18	—	2.47	—	2.05	—
2	3.05	—	2.73	—	2.43	—
3	3.33	3.25	2.78	2.43	2.57	2.11
4	3.96	4.12	3.63	3.29	2.98	2.73
5	4.14	4.51	3.67	4.08	3.12	2.64
6	4.77	5.06	4.33	4.18	3.46	3.12
7	5.36	5.62	4.38	4.07	3.94	3.36
8	5.48	6.22	4.95	6.05	4.24	4.89
9	5.70	6.41	5.16	5.25	4.16	4.33
10	5.93	7.15	5.11	6.79	4.22	5.40
11	6.80	6.38	5.75	5.97	4.92	5.72
12	6.92	8.51	6.05	7.84	5.41	6.11

spontaneous expression—plus more time to reflect on how to express oneself—results in more complicated expressions for the High group. However, for the Low group, the pattern is slower to develop. From grades four through seven, they tend to use more elaboration in oral language than in written language, and *then* go through a transition which follows the High group pattern (more elaboration in written than in oral language). Apparently, learning to write in a way that uses a large repertoire of syntactical strategies develops more slowly for those who lack proficiency in oral language. Very plausibly, they need to develop and practice syntactical complexities in speech before they can use them in writing. In the case of the Random group, this development of oral elaboration as a preliminary to written elaboration is easy to observe by studying the velocity of both the oral and written data.

Transformational Analysis

Six subjects were chosen for the transformational analysis: two each (one boy and one girl) from the High, Random, and Low groups.[19] Each subject was chosen as *typical of his or her group* (see Table 19). The following analysis reveals the implications we found:

1. Both in the first three years of elementary school and the last three years of high school, the High subjects use more trans-

Table 19

Tranformational Analysis: Summary of Overall Totals[a]

Transformations	Early Years						Late Years					
	High		Random		Low		High		Random		Low	
	Male	Female	Male	Female	Male	Female	Male	Female	Male	Female	Male	Female
Single-base	45	19	17	21	17	21	42	25	32	31	31	21
Multi-base (full)	25	15	9	9	13	15	54	50	19	40	30	24
Multi-base (deletion)	34	37	32	30	17	12	46	49	41	33	34	16
Total	104	71	58	60	47	48	142	124	92	104	95	61

Total Transforms

		Early Years	Late Years	Total
Boys plus Girls	High	175	266	441
	Random	118	196	314
	Low	95	156	251
	All Boys	209	329	538
	All Girls	179	289	468

[a]Using two high subjects, two random subjects, and two low subjects for grades one, two, and three and grades ten, eleven, and twelve with a total of 180 units per subject (30 units × 6 grades).

formations than the Random subjects and almost twice as many transformations as the Low subjects.
2. Typically the boys use more transformations than the girls, but this is not true of the Random group in high schools.
3. Note the results on the multi-base deletion transforms in Table 19. We are especially interested in these as examples of closely coiling thought into a minimum of speech, an elegant parsimony:[20]

All Subjects	Early Years	Late Years
High	71	95
Random	62	74
Low	29	50

Although the Low subjects do progress, they are still, during the high school years, producing only about half as many multi-base deletion transforms as the High subjects. Even more striking is evidence that in their last three years of high school, the subjects low in language proficiency were not using as many multi-base deletion transforms as the other two groups were using in grades one, two, and three.

Study of Verbs

From reading scholarly publications dealing with the English verb system,[21] we had concluded that complex verb phrases like the following would be a mark of proficiency with verbs:

He *will have prepared* a notice.
He *had been preparing* a notice.
I got Kevin *to persuade her to ask Jack to change* his mind.
Gail *expected to have been waiting* for hours.
By the time he reaches Baton Rouge, he *will have been driving* for three hours.

As the evidence shows, however, such forms—called catenatives—were seldom used by our subjects, and the groups we studied showed no differences on this use of complex verb phrases. Perhaps our interview situation did not sample this kind of language. Strategies to elicit such language could be ingeniously devised, and it is still our feeling that the differences found would be significant.

Allen's study of verbs used in drama, fiction, and nonfiction found only 4.3% of written verb forms to be such expanded verbs.[22] Apparently expanded verb forms are not commonly used.

Do all native speakers of English have these forms as part of their language competence? We still do not know the answer, but the problem seems important.

As we view the matter now, it appears to us that the situations we used for speech and writing were not sufficient to elicit complex verb phrases or unusual tenses of the verb. What is necessary for this purpose would be a more ingenious set of questions designed to force—if the competence exists—the production of these (presumably) more sophisticated strategies with verbs. For instance, Watts devised tests based on expanded verb forms like the past perfect and future perfect:
Choose the word or words needed to make good sense and cross out the others:

After we $\left\{\begin{array}{l}\text{have had}\\ \text{had had}\\ \text{had}\end{array}\right\}$ supper, the fireworks began.

If I $\left\{\begin{array}{l}\text{have had}\\ \text{had had}\\ \text{had}\end{array}\right\}$ the money I would have paid you.

Watts' test was one in which the pupils read the printed sentences. For the 1980s a fairer test would elicit responses orally with tapes or cassettes.

From our research we still aren't sure if the management of time through verbs is mainly a matter of chronological development or requires powers and strategies that not all speakers possess but might learn if their attention were focused on the skill.

For the present investigation, using the thirty sequential communication units for each subject, we also obtained data on verb density and on the proportions of finite and nonfinite verbs out of total verbs.[23]

Verb Density—Oral and Written Language

In this research each individual verb word was counted separately. For example, if a subject says "I ran," the verb count is one; if he or she says "I would have gone," the verb count is three. For any given grade, each subject's total verb words were tabulated and a calculation made to obtain the measure of *verb words as a percentage of words in communication units*.[24]

From looking at the data, the reader can see that the findings are completely negative (see Table 20). In other words, verb density does not appear to distinguish among the groups, and this is true not only for oral language but also for written language. There does not seem to be any growth in verb density nor is there any consistent pattern other than a very slight percentage superiority of verb density in written language as compared to oral language. However, even this generalization does not always hold true; we find, in both oral and written language, that on the measure of verb density the High group sometimes exceeds the Low group, the Low group sometimes exceeds the High group, and the Random group sometimes exceeds both the High and Low groups. We had expected verb density to show a difference between High and Low groups but the evidence proves otherwise.

Table 20

Verb Words as a Percentage of Words in Communication Units

Grade	Oral			Written		
	High Group	Random Group	Low Group	High Group	Random Group	Low Group
1	21.89	22.76	24.12	—	—	—
2	21.81	22.75	23.66	—	—	—
3	21.77	22.46	22.57	—	—	—
4	21.73	22.03	22.29	24.30	23.80	21.56
5	21.45	22.14	22.97	23.75	23.61	20.92
6	20.94	21.51	22.43	23.18	24.79	19.73
7	21.01	21.60	22.12	22.45	24.67	23.92
8	20.00	21.37	21.54	21.79	22.33	22.32
9	20.55	21.03	22.38	21.74	22.74	21.57
10	21.05	23.01	22.97	21.44	23.38	23.74
11	21.60	22.62	22.66	22.06	24.40	24.31
12	21.11	21.59	22.72	21.86	22.72	22.98

Nonfinite Verbs as a Percentage of Total Verbs—Oral and Written Language

A word of caution: The reader should have clearly in mind exactly what is being measured. In the previous section, we examined total verb words as a percentage of all words in units and found that approximately one word in five is a verb word (roughly 20% although in some cases it was closer to 25%). In the present analysis we are concentrating on nonfinite verbs as a percentage of total *verbs* (not total *words* in units). Therefore, a figure of 10% would indicate that 10% of the *verb* words are nonfinite and the remaining 90% are finite.

Examining the oral data on nonfinite verbs, the first clear feature one notices is that both the High and Low groups exhibit a measurable but erratic growth from the early years to the late years. (See the top portion of Table 21.) However, the growth for both groups is limited to gerunds and infinitives, with relatively constant percentages for participles. An additional feature of the data is that in the late years the Low group actually tends to use a greater proportion of infinitives than the High group. Infinitives appear to be a common and easy syntactical form of expression.

Table 21

Nonfinite Verbs as a Percentage of Total Verbs

	Oral							
	Participles		*Gerunds*		*Infinitives*		*Total*	
Grade	*High Group*	*Low Group*	*High Group*	*Low Group*	*High Group*	*Low Group*	*High Group*	*Low Group*
1	3.20	3.05	0.56	0.60	2.56	1.62	6.32	5.27
2	3.57	2.63	0.50	0.52	1.55	1.76	5.62	4.91
3	3.31	3.72	0.83	0.77	1.76	2.67	5.90	7.16
10	2.51	3.05	0.94	1.07	3.22	3.83	6.67	7.95
11	2.45	2.83	2.61	2.40	4.17	5.03	9.23	10.26
12	3.09	3.01	3.16	2.46	3.66	5.08	9.91	10.55
	Written							
10	4.13	1.36	3.22	2.26	4.53	2.38	11.88	6.00
11	3.57	1.63	2.54	0.72	4.52	4.22	10.62	6.57
12	4.47	2.60	4.14	2.28	5.08	3.46	13.68	8.33

In reality, the difference between the High and Low group is not particularly large. (For example, in grade twelve the *Total* column indicates High = 9.91% and Low = 10.55%.) Therefore, our only conclusion is that on *oral* language the proportions of nonfinite verbs do not distinguish between those rated high and those rated low in language proficiency.

However, when examining *written* language, we find two notable phenomena: (1) the High group demonstrates an obvious percentage superiority over the Low group; and (2) the oral and written data actually move in *opposite* directions, with the High group showing substantially more nonfinite verbs in written than in oral language and the Low group showing substantially more nonfinite verbs in oral than in written language. From this observation we may conclude that those rated high in language make a conscious effort to use nonfinite verbs in their writing whereas those rated low in language do not make such a conscious effort. In written language, the Low group does not fully use the nonfinite verbs they employ in oral language; their performance does not reflect their competence.

In the history of the English language, the use of nonfinite verbal constructions has been increasing for the last five centuries. They are a way of simplifying, and they are forceful; they help us to express and to subordinate thought effectively and directly. It was believed, when this study was initiated, that nonfinite verbs might be a way of identifying the most proficient users of English among the subjects in this study. However, all groups use infinitive constructions orally with about comparable frequency. The High group shows evidence of using these effective forms more frequently only in written composition.

Nonfinite verbs have apparently become so much a part of the people's language that they are easily handled. Because they coil expression of thought more tightly, an instinctive preference for their use may be operating in oral expression. We do not have enough evidence in our study to deal with the use of participles and gerunds. However, one of our doctoral students became interested in the problem. Comparing low and high socioeconomic subjects in grades 6 and 11 on the use of nonfinite verbs, Green found no significant differences either in writing or in speaking.[25]

The search for strategies in which proficient users of language handle verbs more effectively than those not proficient will need to continue. Aspects of effectiveness with verbs other than verb density and the use of nonfinite verbs should be investigated. Perhaps the use of exact and vivid verbs, such as *strolled across the street* instead of *went across the street*, may be one such area for study.

CHAPTER FIVE

CONCLUSIONS

The research reported in this monograph is concerned with the stages, velocity, and relative growth of children's language. The study uses data obtained during an intensive, thirteen-year longitudinal study.

This is a status study, meant to develop baselines to show language development. It is not a study in which any group is given a special treatment in contrast to some other control group. The research did not in any way provide special intervention. The subjects started in eleven kindergartens and gradually spread out to 72 public, parochial, and private schools in a 100-mile radius beyond which, if they moved, we reluctantly abandoned them. Their education was that of typical American children in an urban area.

The major questions forming the purposes and dimensions of the investigation were:

- What are the differences between those who use language effectively and those who do not?
- Does growth in children's language follow predictable sequences? Can stages and velocity of language development be identified for these subjects?

Differences between Effective and Less Effective Subjects

On rating scales used for thirteen years, the 35 subjects who were rated high excelled the 70 typical and low subjects in *control* of ideas expressed. They had an overview, a plan for their talk and writing that showed coherence and unity. They spoke not only freely, fluently and easily, but also effectively, using a rich variety of vocabulary. They adjusted the pace of their words to their listeners, and their inflection or "imparting tone" was adapted both to the meaning of their content and to the needs of their listeners. They were, themselves, attentive and creative listeners.

The less effective subjects rambled without apparent purpose, seemingly unaware of the needs of the listener. Their vocabulary was meager, and as listeners they did not focus on relationships or note how main ideas control illustrations or subordinate ideas. Their writing was disorganized, and they were painful "decipherers" rather than fluent readers.

In the elementary school, the members of the High group were superior in tentativeness or flexibility of expression; they avoided the flat dogmatism of the Low group, the stark statement without possibility of qualification or supposition. They used more subordination than the Low group, thus reducing the number of communication units by combining them in complex fashion. Even so, the High group *still exceeded* the Low group in number of communication units in oral language. Also, the proficient speakers were superior, at a statistically significant level, in smooth, fluent speaking style as opposed to a hesitant, faltering, and labored style of speech.

Although all subjects knew and used all the basic structural patterns of the English sentence, the High group had a much greater flexibility and repertoire *within the pattern of a sentence*; that is, they had more ways to fill slots like the subject, the modifiers, the objects. Their usage was also more conventional than the rest of the subjects.

Both in reading and in written composition, the proficient subjects excelled, and they were superior in using connectors—like *meanwhile, unless*—in a test which showed their median to be almost double that of the Low group. This test was further substantiated by the findings on the use of adverbial clauses of concession and condition where the High group excelled again. On listening tests, those who were superior with oral language ranked highest. It is of special note that those superior in oral language in kindergarten and grade one *before they learned to read and write* are the very ones who excel in' reading and writing by the time they are in grade six. Our data show a positive relationship of success among the language arts.

In addition to the ratings by teachers, we have selected certain features of language and followed their development in the speech and writing of 211 subjects who began as children in kindergarten and ended as young adults thirteen years later. We have been concerned with eight features. The first three deal with fluency in speech and writing:

- average number of words per communication unit
- expansion of subject and predicate (syntactical elaboration)
- freedom from hesitations, language tangles, and unnecessary, unintended repetitions (mazes) in speaking.

The remaining five deal with the use of syntactical strategies:

- grammatical transformations—especially multiple-base deletion transformations
- use and length of dependent clauses
- use of various kinds of dependent clauses
- use of nonfinite constructions, a more direct and tighter form of coiling thought as compared to dependent clauses
- verb density, e.g., proportion of verbs in relation to other words in a communication unit.

Fluency

Readiness and smoothness of speech are a part of proficiency with oral language. A parallel fluency appears in the writings of such men as Walt Whitman or Winston Churchill, poets and leaders whose written and oral language excels that of the average person. Obviously fluency without coherence or veracity can be a vice rather than a virtue, but the ability to find words with which to express oneself—and to find them readily—is normally one mark of success with language. Our three indices of fluency are more empirical and objective than we would prefer, but they do vary definitely and positively with the teacher ratings of the deeper powers of fluency, such as wealth of ideas expressed easily and effectively. The subjects who rank high on average number of words per communication unit and low on language tangles are the ones who speak and write with vivacity and are successful in communicating their meaning. They are capable of both simplicity and impressive elaboration. Those whose syntactical expansion of subject and predicate ranks low are also those who do not use an "imparting tone" in speaking and are weak in organizing their content to evoke understanding in others. Spontaneity and sensitivity to the listener's needs are not among their strengths. Their words are thrown out with vague and undetermined meanings.

In oral language, on average number of words per communication unit, the three groups (High, Random and Low) all show increases, but the High group is at least five or six years in advance of the Low group during all the years of the study. For instance, not until grade six does the Low group attain the level the High group *had already reached in grade one*. The Low group, even though using shorter communication units, nevertheless produces more mazes than the other two groups. In writing, the High group is again more fluent in terms of average number of words per communication unit. The Low group is in the tenth grade before it achieves even the fourth-grade level of the High group.

The reader should note in Figures 1, 4, 5, 7, 13, and 14 how the three groups remain in the same relative positions throughout the years of the study. Oral control of the language, undoubtedly given less attention by instruction, increases regularly. The average number of words per communication unit in writing shows some plateaus and spurts of growth in the secondary schools. Between grades 9 and 10 all groups make a dramatic spurt; after that the Low group remains stationary, but the Random and High groups, after a drop from grades 10 to 11, make another dramatic rise in their last year of school. On all these matters, the Random group typifies the attainment of average urban pupils. Educators concerned with curriculum and evaluation in the language arts should find these results particularly useful.

What do the members of the High group do to extend their communication units beyond the length of the other two groups? What strategies of elaboration do the Random and Low group members employ? First of all, in oral language, those who are rated highly proficient use more dependent clauses, longer dependent clauses and more adjective clauses than the other two groups. They also use the more unusual syntactical elements such as appositives, objective complements, and dependent clauses or nonfinite verb clusters embedded within dependent clauses.

In the written use of dependent clauses, the Random and Low groups catch up with the High group in grades 10, 11, and 12, but this phenomenon results from the fact that the High group has moved to a more sophisticated strategy of replacing cumbersome dependent clauses with more efficient subordination (infinitive phrases and clauses, participle and gerund phrases, appositives, as well as noun, verb and adjective clusters used in cumulative sentences).[1]

Dependent clauses are not the only means by which speakers and writers expand the basic elements of a sentence. Consequently, we also examined all the expansion devices used in the subjects' oral and written communication units. Quantifying the amount of total elaboration, we found the High group again five or six years in advance of their chronologically similar schoolmates in the Low group. For instance, in oral language the High group in the first grade demonstrates a proficiency in elaboration attained by the Low group only at grades five and six, and in grade twelve the Low group has merely reached the eighth-grade level of the High group. One unusual feature, though, is the series of surges and recessions in the written language of the Random group (see Figure 14).

To interpret fluency appropriately, we need to recall how the groups were selected. For thirteen years all their language arts and English teachers rated them on such matters as organization, control, and communicative skill. We then averaged the ratings and from the averages selected the 35 subjects who rated highest in language proficiency over the total period of thirteen years. Next we selected 35 subjects who were lowest in language proficiency. Then we selected, by a table of random numbers, a cross section of 35 subjects. Having chosen these three groups from the 211 subjects on whom we had data for all thirteen years, we then turned back through the years and studied their language development from kindergarten through grade twelve. Thus, it is important to know that those who are rated the highest over a period of thirteen years are the ones who do use more words, greater syntactical elaboration, and fewer mazes at each grade level. Mere counting of such items would be useless if these countings and findings did not relate definitely to power and effectiveness with language.

Inasmuch as fluency connotes a flow of language, its success can be marred by too many hesitations, false starts, and nonfunctional repetitions. Because these language tangles very much resemble the physical behavior of a person seeking a way out of a maze, we called them *mazes* at the beginning of our research, and the name stuck. We defined *maze* as a series of words (or initial parts of words), or unattached fragments which do not constitute a communication unit and are not necessary to the communication unit.

It is only in speech that these language tangles occur, and if one listens attentively to anyone's oral language, or indeed one's own, it soon becomes apparent that the phenomenon is universal. Obviously, it appears to be related to the problems of putting thought and feeling into words, what might be called verbal planning. In writing, one can pause as long as desired, crossing out extraneous words or bungled phrases, thus eliminating mazes.

One cannot listen to these recordings or read the transcripts without noting how frequently the subjects, when they attempt to express themselves, become confused or tangled in words. This confusion occurs not only in interview situations but also in the daily talk of the children, in the classroom when they share experiences, and on the playground of the school. Sometimes the mazes are very long, consisting of from ten to twenty or more words or fragments of words. Sometimes the subjects persevere with the ideas they are trying to formulate and, at the end of the maze, do achieve a unit of communication. Other times the subjects abandon the ideas they are trying to express, perhaps finding the problem too difficult or too tiring to express, or not worth the effort. It is entirely possible that in another situation, where the motivation was much greater, the same idea represented in the maze might find its way to a clear expression of meaning. The energy level or the health of the subject may also be decisive factors in the child's success or failure in converting an idea into a genuine unit of communication.

Mazes are an important but elusive element of speech. Are they related to personality? To self-confidence or insecurity? How much does the social situation influence them? The research of Goldman-Eisler and that of Lawton[2] shows that hesitation pauses vary with the language task: group discussion differs from individual interview, description produces fewer hesitations than abstraction. Hesitation pauses become more frequent as more complex verbal planning is required, as in abstract analysis. Hesitation pauses also precede lexical words more often than function words and they precede the least redundant elements of the sentence syntax more often than the easier redundancies. Bernstein finds that working class adolescent boys are more fluent than middle class boys—e.g., they use fewer hesitation pauses when they are in a discussion situation with one another, using their usual code of speech which is more concrete, descriptive, and narrative than analytical and abstract. (Both groups discussed capital punishment and intelligence scores were held constant.)[3]

Inasmuch as the British researchers have found that situation and social class background influence hesitations, it will be important to look at our mazes in relation to these two features. The subjects in our study were in a situation that can be designated as an individual interview, with no deliberate stimulus for abstract analysis. As to socioeconomic status, our High group is definitely drawn from high economic background with a few from average circumstances; the Low group is from low socioeconomic conditions with a few drawn from average economic background. In our study the High group shows a lesser degree of maze behavior than either of the other two groups.

All groups end at grade twelve with virtually the same percentage of maze words and hesitations they had in grade one, despite the fact that increasing chronological age has produced an increasing complexity in the language of all groups. In relation to the High group, the Low group uses communication units that are short; this emphasizes the fact that the High group consistently has a lower average number of maze words per communication unit. This seems to be the opposite of Bernstein's findings—his working class boys had fewer hesitation phenomena. The explanation may be that his adolescents were in discussion groups composed of their own socioeconomic status, whereas in our study the subjects were expressing themselves to an adult in an individual interview.

Logically, and now empirically, it does look as if situation played a large part in maze behavior. Also because the proportion of mazes to communication unit stays so remarkably stable throughout our study whereas the other language features show change, we wonder if it may be related to an interaction between psychological security and language rather than to chronological language development. Mazes are certainly a curious and interesting feature of language. They are also an important part of fluent communication, and therefore deserve continued study and research in psycholinguistics.

Effectiveness

Now we need to examine even more rigorously how these strategies of subordination contribute to the effective use of language. First we will try a recent theory of language known as transformational or generative grammar. Can the choice of one syntactic structure over another and the idea of hierarchy in syntax be related to creative and effective language use? For this purpose, we chose a typical boy and girl from each of our groups and asked a scholar of transformational grammar to analyze the syntax of these six subjects in grades 1-2-3 and 10-11-12. At both levels the high-rated proficient speakers used more transformations than the nonproficient couple. On multi-base deletion transformations, the results for each couple in oral language were:

	Grades 1,2, and 3	Grades 10,11, and 12
High	71	95
Random	62	74
Low	29	50

Although the Low subjects do progress, they are still, during the high school years, producing only about half as many multi-base deletion transformations as the High subjects. Even more surprising, they are not, even in high school, using as many of these transformations as the other two groups were using in grades 1, 2, and 3. It is striking that in grades 10, 11, and 12, subjects who rank high on every other measure of language proficiency also rank above the Random group by about 25% and above the Low group by about 50% on this skill.

Next we will review the use of dependent clauses. They can be cumbersome rather than effective: "My greatest ambition is to be a nurse which I have had from when I was a child" might receive a firm score on our elaboration index, but it is scarcely a model of clarity and precision. Nevertheless, there is now enough research in English-speaking countries to demonstrate that subordination is one index of maturity in language.[4] Here we will first be concerned with any evidence of maturity in using dependent clauses. For instance, we know that dependent noun clauses used as objects of the verb are learned early in life and easily used by all speakers. This means we will be more interested in other less elementary uses of the noun clause. The same holds true for the adverbial clause of time; its use is no mark of language maturity. Instead, previous studies direct our attention to the use of adverbial clauses of concession and condition as evidences of maturity.

Certainly the thirty-five subjects rated High in language proficiency do use a greater number of dependent clauses in their oral language. At grade four they have already attained the eleventh-grade score of the Low group! In their writing, the story changes, but there is a reason: the High group is shifting from dependent clauses to more economical and effective varieties of subordination (precise nonfinite structures, appositives and other types of non-clause word clusters, phrases that say the same thing as clauses but do so in fewer words). Thus by the time the High group reaches the secondary schools, their writing shows no greater incidence of dependent clauses than the other groups; the Low group now begins to use more dependent clauses in writing, but for genuine language power, they are depending too heavily upon such clauses. At the secondary level in writing, they are doing what the High group did in grades 4, 5, and 6.

Of all European languages, the verb system in English is the most subtle and elaborate. It is also a difficult system, and as in all languages it is the part most difficult for foreigners to learn. Its irregular verbs and its annoying habit of adding s to the present-tense verb in the third person singular make for difficulties in learning, whether for the English-speaking child or the foreigner learning English. Intuitively, also, many speakers and writers feel the English verb is the force, the vitality giving life to sentences. Thus it would seem that an examination of our subjects' use of verbs would pay rich dividends. To that end we read numerous books such as *The English Verb* by Martin Joos and *A Linguistic Study of the English Verb* by F. R. Palmer.

The subjects in this study did, indeed, have difficulties with the English verb system. As reported in two earlier monographs,[5] most of the subjects had problems not only with verb usage, but also with sensitivity to clarity and precision of communication in such matters as tense consistency. Those who initially spoke a social class dialect encountered numerous confusions as they added the standard usage as a second dialect.

In the present monograph, we hoped to report new aspects of the verb system. We tested out a theory of some fellow English teachers, the theory that verb density was characteristic of superior writing. We acted on our own hunch that nonfinite verbs might prove to be a key to skill with the English verb system. In neither case did we find any reliable differences between our groups. We feel that our techniques lack sufficient sophistication, that somehow they do not apprehend the linkage between semantics and stylistics and grammar. At any rate, the simple counting of verb density and incidence of nonfinite verbs does not capture any distinctions of language power.

That we found no differences in the use of nonfinite verbs or in verb density still strikes us as logically puzzling. We can understand that "Bob *hates to mow* the lawn" is relatively uncomplicated syntax and that such a locution might easily be within the powers of all speakers. However, we wonder whether or not the same is true of "By now the astronauts *ought to have been orbiting* for two weeks," or "He *expected to have to start tearing down* the motor again."

Three authors of a language textbook, teachers of English, express a similar conjecture.[6] They believe there is some possibility that one distinction between verbally apt students and those less apt is that the former use expanded verb strings. One of these authors, in a letter to this researcher, says:

> Now I'll hazard a few hypotheses. First, I think that only the very able child (verbally) will often use long, expanded verb strings, since each combination used as a notional auxiliary shows much concern for qualification of predication, and as you have already shown (in *The Language of Elementary School Children*, p. 85), tentativeness and qualification are marks of the superior speaker. Furthermore, these complex strings are usually involved in predicating attitudes, intents, motivations, feelings, and the like; hence only the able and sensitive mind will trouble itself with searching out such qualifications.[7]

Our final conclusion is that further research into language situations more varied than ours still needs to be carried out. Perhaps we should have tallied only verb strings of five or more words; in our research we tallied equally everything from *hates to mow* to *expected to have to start tearing down*. It is still our observation that few of our subjects during the elementary school years spontaneously used tenses such as the expanded forms of the past or future perfect, and anyone who has taught English knows that high school students have difficulty in handling tense sequences whether in speech or in writing.

Stages and Velocity of Language Development

Power over language increases through the successive development of control over meaningful forms—for instance, the ability to handle pronouns; the use of grammatical subordination instead of coordination to show relationships more adequately; the accurate and consistent use of verb tenses; the exact use of "connector" words, i.e., conjunctions or conjunctive adverbs, such as *until, although, however*. The rapidity with which these attainments occur and possibly the order in which they occur varies among children. The order, presumably, will be conditioned by the requirements of a particular situation as well as by the successful combinations already mastered by the speaker. Regressions will occur in situations of social threat, and previous accomplishments will require relearning in the setting of new, more complicated expressions. Very likely, the order and duration of these stages of growth will vary with individuals. No precise formula can be imposed on this development of language power, but an accurate description should reveal order and pattern rather than obscure accident. Through research, the relative stages of growth may be determined for individual children, and baselines charted for more effective instruction of all children.

Are there predictable stages and sequences in language growth? When we asked this question at the beginning of our longitudinal study, we had in mind the well-known longitudinal studies of children's physical growth and development, studies carried out at Yale University by Arnold Gesell and Frances Ilg.[8] Usually our findings show a fairly steady growth in oral language in such matters as average number of words per communication unit (Figure 1), average number of dependent clauses per oral communication unit (Figure 5), and total oral elaboration of subject and predicate (Figure 13). In all of these, however, the steady growth during the elementary school years is altered to a slower pace or plateau in grades 7, 8, and 9—sometimes continuing into grade 10—usually followed by a renewal or even greater velocity of growth in the last few years of senior high school.

By velocity we mean the acceleration, deceleration, or stability of development from one year to the next. For instance, in Figure 14 we see the High group showing a remarkable velocity in elaborating their written sentences in grade 12, and we can surmise that these subjects (or their teachers or both) feel on the back of their necks the hot breath of college entrance standards. The same velocity characterizes the typical or random cross sample, but the group low in language proficiency shows no such spurt of linguistic energy.

In written language the plateaus or decelerations tend to occur at grades 8, 9, 10, and 11, a full year later than the comparable oral loss of velocity. (See Figures 4 and 14, Elaboration and Average Number of Words per Communication Unit.) The Random or typical group often moves ahead by spurts and regressions (Figures 1, 4, 8, and especially 6); their velocity in grade 4 is notable in many of our measures. In the use of written dependent clauses, the High group excels on average number of clauses per communication unit from grade 4 to grade 8. However, by grade 8 the Low and Random groups show an exceptional velocity on this measure; furthermore they equal or exceed the High group in grades 9, 10, and 11. Then in grade 12 the High group again spurts ahead with increased velocity. Examination of their compositions reveals that the High group has moved to subordinating by a variety of means: phrases, gerunds, participles, infinitives, appositives, and nominative absolutes. The Low group begins to use many more dependent clauses in ways similar to the High group's use of them at the earlier elementary school period.

In oral language Templin[9] found eight-year-olds using five times as many subordinate clauses as three-year-olds, but the difference varied according to type of clause: eight-year-olds used four times as many adverb clauses, seven times as many noun clauses, and *twelve times as many adjective clauses*. Evidently the ability to use a variety of adjective clauses is a mark of increasing language development.

Our own findings on the growth rate of oral adjectival clauses is extremely interesting (see Figure 11). The three groups grow apart dramatically, with an amazing surge of velocity taking place for all groups in junior high. Then in grade 9 the Low group falls back, in grade 10 the Random and High groups fall back, but in grades 11 and 12 the High group makes another enormous surge of growth until their incidence of adjectival clauses is more than twice that of the Low group and far above the Random group.

In written composition, the adjective clause has impressed both Lawton and Hunt as a significant feature indicating language development. Using the total number of written adjective clauses in grade 12 as 100%, Hunt found fourth graders using 46%, eighth graders using 68%, and twelfth graders using 100%.[10] Hunt also studied superior adult writers. Comparing them with his subjects, he says: ". . . the increase in number of adjective clauses is most important as an index of maturity. . . . The likelihood that a fourth grader will embed an adjective clause somewhere in a T-unit is only 1 in 20. The likelihood that a superior adult (writer) will do so is 1 in 4."

Drawing up a valid age chart of sequence and stages is hazardous; at any one age children vary tremendously in language ability. However, a picture that may have some usefulness can be constructed from combining our own findings with those of Watts in England, Hunt in Florida, and O'Donnell, Griffin, and Norris in Tennessee.[11] When we do so our result looks like the following.

Ages 5 and 6

Children at this stage settle their use of pronouns, and also of verbs, in the present and past tense, using the inflections of their family. Complex sentences appear more frequently. As early as age two, "pre-forms" of conditionality and causality occur in which the ideas expressed by *why, because* and *if* are implicit in the children's language:

conditionality:
Turn on dat, dat be hot.
You eat your dinner, you have banana.

causality:
Janet don't need a coat on. Janet's too warm a coat.
Don't sit on 'at radiator—very hot.
I can't (come) now. I dus' dettin' dwessed.[12]

In speech, the average number of words per communication unit will be about 6.8 with a range between 6 and 8 for those who speak with weak or strong oral proficiency. The Tennessee research found slightly higher scores, about 7 as an average with a range of 4 to 9.5. Their subjects represent a somewhat more affluent socioeconomic background than those in our Oakland study.

Ages 6 and 7

Further progress occurs in speaking complex sentences, especially those using adjectival clauses. Conditional dependent clauses, such as those beginning with *if* appear. The average number of words per oral communication unit will be about 7.5 with a variation between 6.6 and 8.1. The research group known as High Scope found the average number of words per communication unit in writing, grade two, ranging from 6.9 to 8.3.[13]

Ages 7 and 8

Children can now use relative pronouns as objects in subordinate adjectival clauses (I have a cat *which* I feed every day). Subordinate clauses beginning with *when, if,* and *because* appear frequently. The gerund phrase as an object of a verb appears (I like washing myself). The average number of words per communication unit in oral language will be about 7.6 with a variation between 7 and 8.3 for low and high proficiency children. Far West Laboratory found third-grade writers using 6 and 7 words as the average for communication units.[14]

Ages 8, 9, and 10

Children begin to relate particular concepts to general ideas, using such connectors as *meanwhile, unless, even if.* About 50% of the children begin to use the subordinating connector *although* correctly. They begin to use the present participle active: *Sitting up in bed, I looked around.* The perfect participle appears: *Having read Tom Sawyer, I returned it to the library.* The gerund as the object of a preposition appears: *By seeing the movie, I didn't have to read the book.*

The average number of words per communication unit in oral language will be 9 with a variation from 7.5 to 9.3. The average number of words per T-unit (communication unit) found by Hunt in the writing of subjects this age was 8.1 for boys and 9.0 for girls. The average number of words per written communication unit in our study was 8.0 with a range from 6 to 9. Our figures and Hunt's are similar, as the reader can see. The Tennessee scores also circle around the average of 8.9 for these years, although their variation from weak to strong writing is, as usual, greater than ours.

If twelfth grade is used as a base for the total growth of written adjective clause incidence, then fourth graders have achieved 46% of their total growth on this usage (Hunt).

Ages 10, 11, and 12

At this age children frame hypotheses and envision their consequences. This involves using complex sentences with subordinate clauses of concession introduced by connectives like *provided that, nevertheless, in spite of, unless.* Auxiliary verbs such as *might, could,* and *should* will appear more frequently than at earlier stages of language development. They have difficulties in distinguishing and using the past, past perfect, and present perfect tenses of the verb, and almost none of them use the expanded forms of the past perfect or the future perfect.

Adverbial clauses occurred twice as frequently in the speech of twelve-year-olds as in kindergarten in O'Donnell's research. It was also at this stage that immature coordination of main clauses showed a marked decrease in both speech and writing. This immature command of the resources of language was the primary reason for the adoption of communication units and T-units in language research.

The stage of thinking *if this, then (probably) that* is emerging in speech, usually applied to temporal things rather than to nontemporal ideas and relations: *If* the cost of higher education escalates, *then (probably)* enrollment will falter.

All students in schools show a marked advance in using longer communication units and in the incidence of subordinate adjectival clauses, both in speech and in writing. Nouns modified by a participle or participial phrase appear more frequently than heretofore. So also do the gerund phrase, the adverbial infinitive, and the compound or coordinate predicate: *We* examined and ate *the candy in the package*.

The average number of words per spoken communication unit will be about 9.5 with a variation from 8 to 10.5. The average number of words per written unit in our study was 9 with a range from 6.2 to 10.2, depending upon the child's verbal proficiency.

   With so many scholars now interested in language—in psychology, education, anthropology, linguistics, English, rhetoric, child development, and philosophy—stages like these should be increasingly verified and augmented. We remind the reader again that our charts very often show a steady nondramatic chronological development. This would indicate that linguistic "stages" are no more discrete, no more sudden, than the stages of physical growth reported by Gesell and Ilg. However, if on our charts and figures one examines primary school language development and then compares it with grades 7 to 9 or grades 10 to 12, the degree of development is as apparent as physical growth.

School districts wishing to evaluate language development with more sophistication than published tests provide will find further valuable guidance in the articles and publications of Hunt and the Tennessee research team.[15] In addition, we offer recommendations for such evaluation at the close of Appendix E in this monograph.

In Appendix D the reader may study excerpts from some of the subjects' oral and written language at the same age. We have arranged them to represent the same subject at ages six (eight for written work), twelve, and seventeen.

Socioeconomic Status and Language

There is one aspect of this research—and of almost all recent research on language—that is controversial and also central. Reviewing the composition of the three groups (see Table 1), the reader will note that although various ethnic backgrounds are included in all three groups, the same is not true of socioeconomic backgrounds. The High group is definitely skewed in the direction of the most favored socioeconomic conditions; the Low group is drawn from the least favored.

By now, many studies can be listed to confirm a relation between socioeconomic status and language. To choose one from the many, McClellan selected 200 written compositions at random from those of more than 1000 children in grades three through six. He found that with almost every language factor selected, the higher the socioeconomic level of the writer the better the performance.[16] This finding is typical, and of course it emerges again in the present study as well as in other American studies.

Bernstein, in England, and Poole, in Australia, have both reported research in which working class subjects demonstrate a more restricted use of linguistic strategies than that of middle-class subjects.[17] Bernstein's thesis is that cognitive functioning is mediated by differential language codes according to socioeconomic status. The working-class and middle-class subjects differ in semantic and structural options in the flexibility and specificity with which meanings are expressed and with which abstractions can be successfully communicated. These findings have disturbed many, including linguists who are fully aware of how language has been used in history to sustain closed societies with their rigid class structures. Nor does one need to be a linguist to realize that even in fluid democracies (such as these three English-speaking nations seek to become), where individual worth and aspiration are intended to count for more than affluence or poverty at birth, language still plays an enormous role in economic and social advantage.

An Australian researcher, Millicent Poole, in her *Social Class Contrasts in Linguistic, Cognitive, and Verbal Domains,* has probably summed up the dilemmas and controversies more skillfully than any other writer. She reviews Bernstein and his critics thoughtfully, and then goes on to present her own findings that social class groups can be distinguished in Australian schools by their different patterns of linguistic, cognitive, and verbal functioning. Then she raises the question of whether or not the middle-class styles are really more effective or simply different:

> "If they are more *effective*, the assumption made by the present investigator—probably a heavily value-laden assumption—is that it is desirable and necessary for some students to change so they may gain access to a wider range of linguistic, cognitive, and verbal strategies. This stance assumes, maybe falsely, that the types of intellectual skills which ensure, for example, success at school should be fostered in all children. . . "

Poole then goes on to say that this might well be a false assumption, that the styles may merely be different, that attempting to add styles in children may be a denial of the validity of their own culture. She considers the possibility that it is society as a whole which should change, along with the schools now geared to middle-class achievements and value-orientation, that schools should take cognizance of a more diversified society where a range of language would not only be desirable but also necessary to avert "monolithic cultural and stereotyped patterns." Admitting her affinity to this more diversified vision of society, Poole balances her own point of view with the reality derived from evidence that students with typical linguistic, cognitive, and verbal processing skills have a positive advantage in the society at large as it now exists.

Pondering the thirteen years of experience with over 200 children in Oakland, the present writer concludes that the social conditions we know will continue to exist with gradual modification. Educational preparation for entrance into such a society should include a non-elitist concern with preparation for economic competence: job skills, closer linkage between education and careers, and the option of using informal standard English as a part of that non-elitist preparation for the world beyond schooling. Since, obviously, human beings are not merely economic creatures, the schools should also prepare all pupils in a humanistic curriculum which would reveal not only the beauty and power of all language but also the relation between language and society. The study of language itself should be a central feature in all programs, and schools already including such an emphasis have discovered that not only are students fascinated but they are also stimulated "furiously to think."

Nothing we have ever found supports the idea of any basic ability difference among ethnic groups. What we do find is that those who use the full resources of language usually come from families with reasonably good socioeconomic status. Social injustices, not genetic differences, account most plausibly for the larger number of our minority subjects with lower socioeconomic backgrounds. Anglo subjects from low socioeconomic status fell into the non-proficient language group just as inevitably as the subjects from minority groups.

Some differences in dialect did appear because social-class dialects result from isolation, whether geographic or social, and this accounts for differences in success with the conventional usage of the prestige dialect.[18]

During his work on these transcripts, one of our analysts wrote a thought-provoking comment:

> Every child's language can be assumed to be adequate for his purposes (because if it isn't he will change it) at the given time, and no value judgments should be made based on the complexity of the grammar a child seems to use. There is no *a priori* reason for thinking that the relative complexity of a child's grammar correlates with intelligence, social background, or anything else. Just as every language known in the world is said to satisfy the communicative needs of its users (by definition; if it didn't it wouldn't be complete as a language), so every child's language is adequate for his communicative needs at the moment the language is sampled. This is not a matter of psychology but of linguistic theory and more precisely of the present limitations of linguistic theory.
>
> It amounts to the confession that nothing follows about how to compare two languages with respect to complexity. Complexity viewed as the number of different sentence forms a child can produce seems no more significant than, say, the number of ways in which he can organize a whole group of

sentences. In fact, the number of sentence forms may be a very misleading statistic; every sentence seems to be the result of a large number of steps. This inability of transformational grammar to deal with discourse in general (at the present time) is the opposite side of the coin from the fact that transformational grammar is at present a *sentence* grammar only. In other words, for present purposes, complexity may turn out to be important, and it may not; the issue is an empirical one.

A number of thorny issues reside in this comment. By no means is the world in agreement with the opening sentence, for education in all nations includes language instruction. Nor does every language satisfy the communicative needs of all of its users, even though with time every language can develop strategies to communicate new needs. In the Faroe Islands, the first native language newspaper was published in 1890. "This was the first means by which the public at large learned how to write and express themselves in their own language. But this was not merely learning an orthography. The Faroese vernacular was poor in expressions for abstract conceptions, and a literary language had to be painfully built up, just as an English literary language was built up many centuries ago."[19]

Reflecting on our analyst's caution about the relation of complexity to social background, we, nevertheless, come to the conclusion that in this research complexity *is* related to social background and language proficiency. The group rated high (for thirteen years by large numbers of teachers, each of whom spent a full school year with the pupil) does indeed exhibit more language complexity and greater use of the resources of language. In measure after measure, the subjects whose language power impressed numerous teachers are the ones who show, empirically:

- longer communication units
- greater elaboration of subject and predicate
- more embedding in transformational grammar, especially multi-base deletion transforms
- greater use of adjectival dependent clauses
- more use of dependent clauses of all kinds
- greater variety and depth of vocabulary
- better control of mazes (lower proportion of mazes to total speech)

- higher scores on tests of reading ability
- higher scores on tests of listening
- increasing skill with connectors (*unless, although*, etc.)
- greater use of tentativeness: supposition, hypotheses, conjecture, conditional statements

Some readers may counter that the standards of the Bay Area schools and the expectations of teachers reflect a bias favoring advantaged speakers of standard English. When we look at the list above, we doubt this very much. What is a more plausible explanation? We believe the social conditions under which the high-performance subjects lived provided them with practice in situations requiring and encouraging power of expression. Their home lives and their compatibility with the school environment exacted of them complexity of thought, functional uses of abstraction, distillations of experience into words, and imaginative foreseeing of consequences. Their need for more concepts induced language for categorizing, comparing, contrasting, and conjecturing as well as for clarifying and communicating feelings and emotions. It does seem to us that if all children had similar experiences and similar motives for expression, their language, responding to such challenges, would demonstrate much the same degree of proficiency. Variations would result from psychological and physical factors rather than sociological.

We realize that language is one effective means of maintaining social class stability, certainly *not* one of the aims of education in a democracy. In the closed societies of the past, each class spoke differently, and language was one of the most effective means of maintaining the unchanging nature of those class societies. In Denmark a tart saying illuminates this relation of language to class distinction: "In the old days our Danish nobility spoke French to one another, German to their merchants, and Danish to their dogs." The implications of this saying are not limited to Denmark; we know from history that the favored groups in all nations separated themselves from the masses by means of language. Not always did they use a foreign language; more often they spoke a prestige dialect which differed from the dialect of the peons, peasants, or poor. As long as such societies remain stable, the variations in language cause few problems, support the class society, and stabilize it. In an open society such as ours, education should act to diminish and overcome this ancient element of social control, this extraneous determination of individual destiny. Here, where individual worth and aspiration are intended to count for more than fortunate or unfortunate birth, language still operates to preserve social class distinctions and remains one of the major barriers to crossing social lines. In order for our schools to assist other institutions in making equality of opportunity a reality, teachers need to understand how language and social caste are linked and why many middle-class people naively condemn the language of the least favored economic groups. On attitudes concerning language, teachers can learn much from sociology. We fear nonstandard speech and are inclined to give it no quarter. "The more precarious our social status in the higher classes—that is, the closer we are to the line that divides the middle from the lower classes or the more recent our ascent from the lower strata—the more insistent we are on the purity of our linguistic credentials."[20]

Realizing that human worth cannot be measured by the language or dialect a person uses, teachers will be more likely to help children acquire standard English without making them ashamed of their own way of speaking. Such an addition—not "improvement"—of language options is much more possible through instruction where drill and directed effort are oral and where they are not long separated from language used to express ideas, attitudes, and values of genuine concern to the learners. Not only different usage but also awareness of situation, of how listeners are helped or hindered by one's language, proves to be the need of most learners. To achieve language flexibility pupils must apply whatever is studied to situations in which they have something to say, a deep desire to say it, and someone to whom they genuinely want to say it.

If a little knowledge is a dangerous thing, no one is at present out of danger in the study of language. There is need for many more interested researchers observing children's language in varied situations and making systematic records of that language. Complex truth is always an aggregate; each of us offers only part of an evolving mosaic.

BIBLIOGRAPHY

Allen, Robert L. *The Verb System of Present-Day American English.* The Hague: Mouton & Co., 1966.

Bernstein, Basil. "Language and Social Class." *British Journal of Sociology* 11 (1960): 271-76.

_____. "Linguistic Codes, Hesitation Phenomena and Intelligence." *Language and Speech* 5 (1962): 31-46.

_____. "A Public Language: Some Sociological Implications of Linguistic Form." *British Journal of Sociology* 10 (1959): 311-26.

_____. "Social Class and Linguistic Development: A Theory of Social Learning." In *Education, Economy and Society, A Reader in the Sociology of Education,* edited by A. H. Halsey, Jean Floud, and C. Arnold Anderson, pp. 288-314. New York: Macmillan, Free Press of Glencoe, 1961.

_____. "Social Class, Linguistic Codes and Grammatical Elements." *Language and Speech* 5 (1962): 221-40.

_____. "Some Sociological Determinants of Perception." *British Journal of Sociology* 9 (1958): 159-74.

Bruner, Jerome S.; Goodman, Jacqueline J.; and Austin, George A. *A Study of Thinking.* New York: John Wiley and Sons, 1956.

Fries, Charles C. *American English Grammar.* New York: Appleton-Century-Crofts for NCTE, 1940.

Goldman-Eisler, Frieda. "Speech Analysis and Mental Processes." *Language and Speech* 1 (1958): 59-75.

Harrell, Lester E. "A Comparison of the Development of Oral and Written Language in School-Age Children." *Society for Research in Child Development Monographs* 22 (No. 3). Lafayette, Indiana: Purdue University, Child Development Publications, 1957.

Heider, F. K., and Heider, G. M. "A Comparison of Sentence Structure of Deaf and Hearing Children." *Psychological Monographs* 52 (1940): 42-103.

Hunt, Kellogg W. *Grammatical Structures Written at Three Grade Levels*. Research Report No. 3, Urbana, Ill.: National Council of Teachers of English, 1965.

———. "Recent Measures in Syntactic Development." *Elementary English* 43 (1966): 732-39.

———. "A Synopsis of Clause-to-Sentence Length Factors." *English Journal* 54 (1965): 300-309.

John, Vera P., and Goldstein, Leo S. "The Social Context of Language Acquisition." *Merrill-Palmer Quarterly* 10 (1964): 265-75.

Joos, Martin. *The English Verb: Form and Meanings*. Madison and Milwaukee, Wis.: The University of Wisconsin Press, 1964.

Labov, William. "Stages in the Acquisition of Standard English." In *Social Dialects and Language Learning*, edited by Roger Shuy, pp. 77-103. Urbana, Ill.: National Council of Teachers of English, 1965.

Lawton, Denis. "Social Class Differences in Language Development: A Study of Some Samples of Written Work." *Language and Speech* 6 (1963): 120-43.

———. *Social Class, Language, and Education*. New York: Schocken Books, 1968.

———. "Social Class Language Differences in Group Discussions." *Language and Speech* 7 (1964): 183-204.

Loban, Walter. *Language Ability: Grades Seven, Eight, and Nine*. Washington, D.C.: U.S. Department of Health, Education, and Welfare, Office of Education, OE-30018, Cooperative Research, Monograph No. 18, 1966.

———. *Language Ability: Grades Ten, Eleven, and Twelve*. (Final Report, Project No. 2387, Contract No. OE 4-10-131) Washington, D.C.: U.S. Department of Health, Education, and Welfare, Office of Education, Bureau of Research, 1967.

———. *The Language of Elementary School Children*. Research Report No. 1, Urbana, Ill.: National Council of Teachers of English, 1963.

———. "Language Proficiency and School Learning." In *Learning and the Educational Process*, edited by John D. Krumboltz, pp.113-31. Chicago: Rand McNally & Company, 1965.

———. *Problems in Oral English*. Research Report No. 5. Urbana, Ill.: National Council of Teachers of English, 1966.

_____. "Teaching Children Who Speak Social Class Dialects." *Elementary English* 45 (1968): 592-99; 618.

Minnesota Scale for Paternal Occupations. Institute of Child Welfare. Minneapolis: University of Minnesota Press, n.d.

O'Hare, Frank. *Sentence Combining: Improving Student Writing without Formal Grammar Instruction*. Research Report No. 15. Urbana, Ill.: National Council of Teachers of English, 1973.

O'Donnell, Roy C.; Griffin, William J.; and Norris, Raymond C. *Syntax of Kindergarten and Elementary School Children: A Transformational Analysis*. Research Report No. 8. Urbana, Ill.: National Council of Teachers of English, 1967.

Österberg, Tore. *Bilingualism: And the First School Language—An Educational Problem Illustrated by Results from a Swedish Dialect Area*. Vasterbottens Tryckeri AB-Umea. Sweden. 1961.

Palmer, Frank R. *A Linguistic Study of the English Verb*. London: Longmans, Green and Co. Ltd., 1965.

Piaget, Jean. *The Language and Thought of the Child*. New York: Harcourt, Brace and Company, 1926.

Poole, Millicent. "Comparison of the Factorial Structure of Oral Coding Patterns for a Middle-Class and a Working-Class Group." *Language and Speech* 17 (1974): 222-39.

_____. Review of *Class, Codes and Control*, edited by Basil Bernstein. *Language in Society* 4: 73-84.

_____. "Social Class Differences in Language Predictability." *British Journal of Educational Psychology* 42 (June 1972): 127-36.

_____. *Social Contrasts in Linguistic, Cognitive and Verbal Domains*. Melbourne, Australia: Centre for the Study of Urban Education, La Trobe University, 1975.

Watts, A. F. *The Language and Mental Development of Children*. Boston: D. C. Heath & Company, 1948.

Williams, Frederick, and Naremore, Rita C. "Social Class Differences in Children's Syntactic Performance: A Quantitative Analysis of Field Study Data." *Journal of Speech and Hearing Research* 12 (1969): 778-93.

APPENDICES

APPENDIX A

TEACHERS' EVALUATION OF LANGUAGE SKILL

A rating scale was filled out by the child's teacher at the close of each school year. Thus there are at least thirteen ratings for each subject. However, student teachers, teaching assistants, and multiple teachers at the junior and senior high levels usually lead to more than thirteen ratings per subject.

We averaged the entire series of ratings for all subjects who completed the study. On that basis the High and Low groups of thirty-five members each were selected. The random group was selected according to the usual random numbers technique. Ratings on Activity and on Acceptance-Rejection were not used in selecting the High and Low groups in language proficiency.

Teacher's Evaluation of Language Skill

Name of Pupil_____ Date of Rating _____
              (last name first)   (month)   (year)

Teacher _____

TO TEACHERS

Your help on the following points will be greatly appreciated. In rating each item, disregard your ratings for that pupil on every other item; try not to let general impressions color your judgments about specific aspects of the pupil's language. We would most certainly appreciate any comments, illustrations or noteworthy episodes that throw light on the ratings. If you can give us the time, write them in any empty space or on the last page.

Number 1 is *LOW* and is described by the words at the lefthand side of the scale.

The numbers 2, 3, and 4 represent degrees between HIGH (5) and LOW (1).

Number 5 is *HIGH* and is described by the words at the righthand side of the scale.

PLEASE CHECK BY ENCIRCLING THE NUMBER APPRO-
PRIATE IN EACH CASE.

> EXAMPLE: You consider a pupil just slightly better than av-
> erage on a certain skill. You circle the number
> four, as follows:

$$1\ 2\ 3\ \textcircled{4}\ 5$$

LOW   *HIGH*
1. Skill in communication

incompetent with all lan-
guage; no awareness of
listeners; speaks without
trying to evoke under-
standing from others;
halting pace of words and
inflections of voice not
adjusted to listeners;
writes like an illiterate
person

1 2 3 4 5

uses language in any
form with power, profi-
ciency, and pleasure; ad-
justs pace of words and
inflection to listeners;
uses an "imparting
tone"; is aware of need to
make self understood;
writes competently with
a sense of style

2. Organization, purpose, and point

rambles, no sense of
order or of getting to the
point; rattles on without
purpose; cannot tell a
story or express ideas in a
suitable sequence

1 2 3 4 5

plans what is said; gets to
the point; has *control* of
language; can tell a story
or express ideas in a suitable sequence

3. Wealth of ideas

seldom expresses an
idea; appears dull and
unimaginative; doesn't
originate suggestions or
plans

1 2 3 4 5

expresses ideas on many
different topics; makes
suggestions on what to
do and how to carry out
class plans; shows imagi-
nation and creativity in
many ways

4. Fluency

seldom talks; exception-
ally quiet; needs to be
prompted to talk; *overly*
laconic

1 2 3 4 5

talks freely, fluently, and
easily; also talks bril-
liantly and effectively

5. Vocabulary

uses a meager vocabulary, far below that of most pupils this age; inarticulate, mute	1 2 3 4 5	uses a rich variety of words; has an exceptionally large, effective, and growing vocabulary; speaks fluently with vocabulary suited to listeners

6. Quality of listening

inattentive, easily distrated; seldom attends to the spoken language of others; doesn't listen for relationships or note how main ideas control illustrations or subordinate ideas	1 2 3 4 5	superior attentiveness and understanding of spoken language; a creative listener

7. Quality of writing

lacks coherent organization; often does not follow conventional usage and spelling; a very poor writer	1 2 3 4 5	organizes in terms of a purpose; excludes irrelevant materials; subordinates elements not to be stressed; uses appropriate style, acceptable usage, and conventional spelling; a superior writer

8. Reading

reads only what he has to read; "deciphers" print rather than reads it; gets no ideas from books; will not very likely read more than newspapers and magazines (if that) when schooling is over	1 2 3 4 5	reads voraciously, easily, and with interest books of merit and difficulty; absorbs ideas from books easily and accurately; will undoubtedly read much all throughout life

1. Activity

listless, apathetic, passive; has very little to do with others; prefers to sit; has low energy level; has slow reactions; seems always tired

1 2 3 4 5

very active; relates easily and freely with others; has a high energy level; enjoys physical activity; has quick reactions; seems exceptionally vital and alive

2. Acceptance or rejection

rejected by others, disliked; almost never chosen by others or included in activities; almost entirely isolated

1 2 3 4 5

notably popular with everyone; others seek his or her company; never lacks companionship; always included in peer-group activities

OTHER COMMENTS:

Your comments here on the language or general adjustment of this pupil are most helpful to the research. Any comments will be of great interest to us and deeply appreciated. (Use other side if necessary.)

APPENDIX B

DIRECTIONS FOR ANALYZING TRANSCRIPTS

Miscellaneous Notes: Use pencil for numbers in margins; also use pencil for the slant lines at end of each communication unit. Be sure to write *all* numbers very legibly so the person who adds them will have no trouble. When a transcript is completed, place your initials in the upper right-hand corner of page one.

Counting Words

In counting words in communication units, *yes*, *no* and *uh-huh* are each counted as a single unit if they answer a preceding question. Example:

Units	*Words*	
		Q. Are you going?
2	1/6	A. Yes, / and my mamma is going, too.
1	4	A. Yes, I am going.

Note, however, that if *yes* is closely connected to the rest of the communication unit as in "Yes, I am going," *yes* is counted as part of the following unit.

Units	*Words*	
3	11	I'm gonna get a boy 'cause he hit me./
	13	I'm gonna beat 'im up an' kick 'im in his nose/
	9	an I'm gonna get the girl, too.

Count *gonna* and *I'm* as two words. Note that the first communication unit could not be divided up after *boy* without its essential meaning disappearing. Note in the last two units that a *compound predicate* (beat and kick) results in one unit, but a *compound sentence* (which *can* be divided without essential loss of meaning) becomes two communication units. This is a very important discrimination in this research, and the analyst must be sure to comprehend the distinction.

Count words according to their adult equivalent:

As one word:
    Maybe (perhaps)
    O.K.   (yes)
    ain't   (In this case there was an arbitrary decision to count
             this as one word.)

As two words:
Uptown (to town)	
John Smith	Usta (used to)
Kinda (kind of)	don't
Sorta (Sort of)	haven't
Musta (must have)	(and other common contractions)

As three words:
    S'a   (it is a)
    S'all (that is all)

As four words:
    Dunno (I do not know)
    Un no (I do not know)
    'no   (I do not know)

(Some research groups count these words differently. Do not worry about this matter. When one has enough units for a subject, such minor variations do not affect the ultimate scores.)

Mazes

The analyst is to bracket all mazes in red. Use brackets [ ], *not parentheses* ( ). Using a red pencil, the analyst is to place in the left-hand margin the number of words in the maze. If the maze is obviously and integrally related to a communication unit or a portion of a communication unit, the number of words in the maze and the number of words in the communication unit are both to appear, with a dash connecting them, on the same horizontal level in the margin. If the maze is unrelated to a communication unit, the number of words in the maze appears by itself in the margin. Sometimes the marginal notation will show the maze at the beginning of a communication unit, sometimes in the middle of a communication unit, sometimes at the conclusion of the communication unit. Nonessential petitions and repetitions are counted as mazes. Initial parts of words are counted as half-words.

In these mazes, count an incomplete word as a half-word, whether or not it seems to be the start of a recognizable word. These are entered in red pencil and are entered in the chart as maze words.

Note that when a maze is removed from a unit, the remaining material constitutes a straightforward, acceptable communication unit.

Subordination

In the transcripts, phrases (excluding verb phrases) are underlined twice with a blue pencil; dependent clauses are enclosed in blue parentheses. Over each group is written *adj.* or *adv.* or *noun*, depending on the part it plays in the sentence. Examples:

1. We put the wood <u>on top</u> of the boxes.
   (adv.)   (adj.)

2. We do the things (that they do on television).
                    adj.

3. I think ∧ (that) they're going to kill some animals.
                  noun

4. We like to play London Bridges (if we have enough children).
                                              adv.

Where the subordinate conjunction is understood, as in example 3, write in the omitted word enclosing it in parentheses and indicating the omission by using the caret (∧).

Later analysis of subordination will include designation of first order subordination (subordinate element modifying or completing some part of the independent element) and second order subordination (subordinate element modifying or completing some part of *another subordinate element*).

Special Problems

a. Appositives: the analyst has to exercise judgment in some cases that might be classified either as repetition (a maze) or as apposition. If the same words are used twice—or almost the same words—the analyst should usually consider the material as a maze. Probably the child has barely achieved a communication unit and feels the need to fortify his precarious achievement. Appositives, on the other hand, use different words for the same concept and are counted as part of the longer communication unit.

Units	Words	Examples:
1	(3½)	-4 [Those were - - n - - were]—Those were saucer mens (repetition, a maze)
2	8	They got a fellow there—a young man—/
	6	and his name is Buffalo Bob./ (Appositive, counted as 3 words of an eight-word communication unit.)

b. Mazes unrelated to a coherent unit of communication are counted as zero in the column for units.

Units	Words	Example:
0	(9½)	Then I tol', I tom on the map— ah, ah, uh.

c. If a communication unit is repeated after intervening language, count it as a unit, not as a maze. (This occurs rarely.)

Counting Totals

At the bottom of *each page* of a transcript, place the totals for that page. The number representing total words in mazes and the number of mazes should be in red. The figures should occur in the order shown by the following example:

number of communication units	number of words on page (not counting words in mazes)	mazes	words in mazes
18	114	(4)	(25)

At the very top of the first page, cumulative totals for all of the pages should appear in the same order.

Segmentation

The system of segmenting both oral and written language is explained here. However, the analysis of the oral language transcripts is more difficult and complex, so for that purpose, directions will be given for three kinds of segmentation:[1]

First, the subjects' speech is segmented by patterns of oral intonation, and then units of syntax (each independent predication) are identified within such intonation segments.

- The first of these—intonation pattern—is judged by the contours of inflection, stress, and pause in the subject's voice. Because the segmentation is made in accordance with the sound-system of English, this first and more comprehensive segment is called a *phonological unit.*

- The second unit, usually a subdivision of the phonological unit but sometimes coextensive with it, is called a *communication* unit because it is identified by the meaning being conveyed, as well as the structure of its syntax.

- Beyond these two kinds of segmentation, a third element still remains to be accounted for, an exceptionally interesting and frequent occurrence that can best be described as a tangle of language making no semantic sense and impossible to classify phonologically or semantically. These language tangles have, therefore, been segmented separately and have been labeled *mazes.* Each of these three segments will now be described more fully.

The phonological unit

An example will help to make clear what the phonological unit is. One child in the study said the following words:

> I'm going to get a boy | 'cause he hit me.# I'm going to beat him up and kick him in his nose || and I'm going to get the girl, too.#

The moments of silence, or pauses in the subject's speech, in association with his use of pitch, are shown by the two double-cross junctures (#); this symbol is used to indicate a clear-cut termination to an utterance. Such a termination is usually marked by a definite pause, preceded by a diminishing of force and a drop in the pitch of the voice (or a rise in pitch for queries). The other two marks—the double-bar juncture (||) and the single-bar juncture (|)—represent momentary silences, or pauses of less finality. In this example, the speaker used two definite phonological units, corresponding to the two sentences; these units were characterized by definite pauses preceded by a definite drop in pitch.[2] The phonological unit then is an utterance occurring between the silences represented by double-cross junctures. The phonological units in the example are identical with traditional grammatical "sentences," but the subjects sometimes answered questions in phonological units that were, grammatically, subordinate clauses.

Spontaneous recognition of the phonological units exacts the utmost effort and concentration from whoever is marking them.

Pitch, volume, and juncture are never used as regularly, precisely, and unambiguously as they would be in an ideal linguistic world. The clearest and ablest speakers among the subjects customarily do use intonation with great skill, signaling the endings of their utterances by unmistakably falling pitch, fading volume, and definite pause. Many are not this skilled, however, and furthermore each individual's intonation system is unique; each element of vocal signaling—pitch, pause, stress—is relative to that individual's idiosyncratic ways of speaking. Thus each speaker is a new challenge to the analyst, who must become almost intuitively accustomed to that individual's speed or deliberateness of speaking, ways of breathing, degrees of pitch variation, length of juncture, and amount of stress. Personal styles of impulsiveness, emphasis, and enunciation encircle the basic intonations and influence the analyst-listener. The Gestalt principle, that the elements one perceives are influenced by the ground and field against which they are received, could not be more strikingly exemplified.

The communication unit

The communication unit has been defined by Watts as a group of words that cannot be further divided without loss of their essential meaning. Hunt has called it "the minimal terminal unit."[3] For instance, "I know a boy with red hair" is a unit of communication. If "with red hair" is omitted, the essential meaning of that particular unit of communication has been changed. "I know a boy" does not mean the same thing as "I know a boy with red hair." In all cases, the words comprising a communication unit are either independent grammatical predications or answers to questions which lack only the repetition of the question elements to satisfy the criterion of independent predication. Given this definition, the single word "yes" can be admitted as a whole unit of communication when it is an answer to a question. Thus, communication units prove to be not exclusively semantic; they are also syntactic, being composed of independent predications; they can be identified by their form as well as by their meaning. Since Watts' "essential meaning" might be difficult to define scientifically, a formal definition of the communication unit as "an independent clause with its modifiers" is more defensible than a semantic definition.

The following examples illustrate the method of tallying communication units. A slant line (/) marks the completion of each communication unit. (The # marks the completion of a phonological unit.) Contractions of two words into one are counted as two words.

Examples of Communication Units

Transcript of subject's actual language	Number of communication units	Number of words per units
I'm going to get a boy 'cause he hit me.#/ I'm going to beat him up an' kick him in his nose||/ and I'm going to get the girl, too.#/	3	11 13 9

Note that the first communication unit could not be divided after "boy" without the disappearance of (1) its essential meaning and (2) a subordinate clause that is part of the independent predication. Note in the last two communication units that a compound predicate with the same subject is classified as one unit, but a compound *sentence* (which *can* be divided without essential loss of meanings) becomes two communication units. This distinction is of importance to this study and should be noted carefully by the reader. In grammatical terms, the communication unit in this research generally proves to be an independent clause with its modifiers. No communication unit includes more than one such clause. Thus this second kind of segmentation can actually be achieved structurally, but it is reinforced by the use of meaning.

The maze

One cannot listen to these recordings or read the transcripts without noting how frequently the subjects become confused or tangled in words. This confusion occurs not only in interview situations but also in the daily talk of the children, in the classroom when they share experiences, and on the playground of the school. It is a language behavior consisting of many hesitations, false starts, and meaningless repetitions. It resembles very much the physical behavior of someone trying to find their way out of an actual spatial maze. They thrash about in one direction or another until, finally, they either abandon their goal or find a path leading where they wish to go. Sometimes they stumble upon the path; sometimes they have enough presence of mind to pause and reason out where it is.

A *maze* is defined as a series of words (or initial parts of words), or unattached fragments which do not constitute a communication unit and are not necessary to the communication unit.

Sometimes the mazes are very long, consisting of 10 to 20 or more words or fragments of words. Sometimes the subjects persevere with the ideas they are trying to formulate and, at the end of the maze, do achieve a unit of communication. At other times the subjects abandon the ideas they are trying to express, perhaps finding them too difficult or too tiring to express, or not worth the effort. It is entirely possible that in another situation, with greater motivation, the same idea hinted at in a maze might be clearly expressed. The energy level or the health of the subject may also be decisive factors in the ability to express an idea.

Mazes are not counted as communication units. The procedure has been to count the words in them and then circle this count. When a maze is removed from a communication unit, the remaining material *always* constitutes a straightforward, acceptable communication unit. Furthermore, just as the communication units belong to larger, phonological units, so too do the mazes.[4]

In the written transcripts, only the communication units will occur. Obviously the phonological units are for speech only, and the same is actually true of mazes. Occasionally in writing there will be some language that is garbled, but such garbles do not arise from the same cause as mazes. They should be noted and removed from the written communication unit; however, the analyst will find very few of them.

In the oral language transcipts, the analyst will work only with the communication unit. The typist-transcribers have already used the phonological unit to make their transcriptions. Only occasionally will you, the analyst, need to replay a tape to verify a decision or to untangle a puzzle. The following section explains more fully how the phonological units are used.

When to use phonological units

In practice, phonological units are not regularly identified. Earlier in the study, when the subjects were in the elementary grades,[5] the phonological units were identified and marked, but in grades seven through twelve, these markings were used only when the analyst was puzzled about a maze or a communication unit. Experience has developed in the staff transcribers an exceptional ability to segment the communication units on the typed transcript by listening to the recordings and using intonation as an aid. Occasionally, however, there is some doubt about where a particular communication unit begins or ends. In such cases, the tape is replayed again and again while several analysts listen in order to reach concurrence. In such cases, the phonological markings are carefully made on the transcript.

Frequently, the problem requiring such replaying, careful listening, analyst consensus, and marking occurs when a subject completes an utterance and then adds an afterthought to it. Here are two examples taken from the transcripts:

1. # he looks like he found buried treasure # on that old ship #

2. # it's about these four men # during the Civil War time #

Study of afterthoughts like these reveals that the subjects use a systematic method for linking afterthoughts to a previous utterance: the link is the subject's introduction of the afterthought on the same low voice pitch with which he or she concluded the previous utterance. If we mark for pitch the examples shown above (using 1 for low pitch, 2 for ordinary pitch, and 3 for high pitch), this is what we get:

1. # he looks like he found buried treasure # on that old ship #

2. # it's about these four men # during the Civil War time #

"Low pitch linkage" is characteristic of afterthoughts cast in many types of grammatical construction—prepositional phrases, infinitives, appositives, dependent clauses. Low pitch (1) following the typical sentence intonation pattern, which is (2 3 1) #, is a signal of sentence continuation, whereas ordinary pitch (2) is a signal of new sentence beginning:

he likes to find shells # on the beach he looks for the new ones washed up by the tide

Inasmuch as the main purpose of phonological segmenting in this research is to reinforce and substantiate decisions on communication units, these phonological units are not marked unless real doubt about a communication unit arises. The important aim in segmenting is to establish accurately the communication units and the mazes, since they are the segments that tell the most about growth in language proficiency.

APPENDIX C

DIRECTIONS FOR COUNTING QUOTATIONS

Sometimes when telling a story, a speaker will use what is essentially a direct quotation. Often these quotations consist of more than one sentence and yet are preceded by a single *he says, she asks*, etc. For example: He said, "why don't you come with me? / I am going to the store. / I am going to buy a present." / Although the speaker could have placed *He said* before each communication unit, he attached them all to the one use. Since the second and third units belong with the first *he said*, the entire group is actually a single communication unit. To give the speaker credit for using this construction, count each individual unit and then in addition count the entire construction as another communication unit. Therefore, in the example above the speaker would have a total of four communication units: three for the individual units and one additional for the overall construction—a large communication unit in its own right.

A sample paragraph is given from one speaker's transcript in which he uses several of these constructions. The only difference from previous practice is in the counting of communication units; this does not change the method of counting words, mazes, etc. The individual examples presented here are taken from the sample paragraph. Mazes have been omitted in these examples in order to focus on the counting of quotations.

Example 1: and he keeps on saying "but Mom, why can't I go down to the lollipop store / I'm so hungry I'm just going to die of hunger / and you wouldn't want me to die of hunger would you" / (4 units)

Example 2: and his mother says "now don't be ridiculous / you know you're eating an orange / and how can you starve to death while you're eating an orange? / (4 units)

Example 3: and so Johnny said "well if I weren't may I go down to the lollipop store" / (1 unit)

Example 4: and she said "no you've been down to the lollipop store too many times this week" / (1 unit)

Example 5: and so Johnny said "but Mom, I'd dust the floors /
and I'd clean the windows / and I'd mop out the
basement / and I'd brush the horse" / (5 units)

Example 6: and she said "stop it / you're tempting me" / (3 units)

Example 7: and then she said "all right you may go / but you'll
have to do all the work" (3 units)

This count only applies, of course, if there is more than one
communication unit within the *total* quotation. Examples 3 and 4
above have a total count of one because there is only one unit
following the introductory words (and she said, and so Johnny
said). Therefore, watch for words indicating a quotation will follow. Every time one of these words appears (said, says, asks, etc.),
a new communication unit starts and the quotations following go
within that unit. Remember to add the extra unit every time this
type of quotation structure occurs.

In computing the average number of words per communication
unit, count the words in each unit. Add your totals and divide by
the number of units. This is the average. Then, assign this average
to the unit representing the total quotation. For instance, in example 7 above, the first unit contains 9 words and the second unit
contains 9 words. The overall unit, therefore, is an average of the
two units: 9+9 divided by 2 = 9. In this case the subject received
credit for three units of 9 words each.

Sample — How to Count Quotations

Words in Units and Mazes	
7	This is a little boy named Johnny / and [he-] he is sitting on the
1-①-10	
④-8-①-8	front porch looking very glommy / [and he- and he-] and he's very
①½-13	
	angry with his mother [because] well because he can't go down to [the
	lolli-] the lollipop store and buy a lollipop or maybe an ice cream cone /
17	and he keeps on saying "but Mom, why can't I go down to the lollipop
12	store / I'm so hungry I'm just going to die of hunger / and you
12	wouldn't want me to die of hunger would you" / [and she-] and his mother
②-5-③-4	says "now [don't be-] don't be ridiculous / you know [you- you-]
2-②-5	
13	you're eating an orange / and how can you starve to death while you're
2-①-3-②-	eating an orange? / and so [Johnny] Johnny said "well [if I-] if I
4-②-8	weren't [may I-] may I go down to the lollipop store" / and she said

Words
in Units
and Mazes

4-③-13	"no [you've been-] you've been down to the lollipop store too many
②-11	times this week" / [and so-] and so Johnny said "but Mom, I'd dust the
6	floors / and I'd clean the windows / and I'd mop out the basement /
7	
③-6	[and I'd-] and I'd brush the horse" / and she said "stop it / you're
5	
4	tempting me" / [so- so she- she] and then she said "all right you may
④-9	
9	go / but you'll have to do all the work" / [so-] so finally Johnny
①-21	
	did it — mopped out the basement and dusted the house, and cleaned the
14-③½-11	windows and brushed the horse / and he was so tired that he just layed
	right down on the couch [and went to sl-] and went to sleep instead of
	going to the lollipop store.

26 Units

APPENDIX D

SAMPLES OF TRANSCRIPTS AND
WRITTEN COMPOSITIONS

Here we have arranged several oral language transcripts and written compositions of three boys, one each from the High, Random, and Low groups. For each of these subjects we have an excerpt from the oral language transcription at ages six, twelve, and seventeen, and we have shown our analysis of communication units, words in communication units, and mazes. We have also shown the analysis for several of the written compositions. Readers who wish to do so can easily divide the number of words by the number of communication units to find the average number of words per communication unit.

Angelo G.
High Proficiency Group
Transcripts of Oral Language

Grade One   **Age Six**
(Answer to "What Makes You Cry?")

2-①-2-②-7	Well, sometimes [he] — my brother — [he. . he] he's kind of a tough guy /
5	
4	and he likes to fight. / He's about four / and [he] sometimes he hits me. / He
1-①-4	
10	used to hit me back here all the time. / And sometimes he plays these funny
9	
8	games with me. / He makes me get down on the floor / [and he stick . and he
7-⑥	
6	makes me] and you know what he does? / He calls this the big hut / and this is
5	
7	big hut / and my back's a big hut / and guess what he calls my [uh] seat / the
6-⑦½-1	
3	big wutty / and [he] he comes along / and he goes, "Big hut, big hut, big hut,
1-①-3	
13	big wutty," like that. / That doesn't exactly make me cry, / but that's one
7	
12	of the things that he does with me / [and he makes me —] and sometimes he
④-9-6	
2-①-11	gets me down on the floor, / and you know what he does? / He sticks [his] his
9	feet up, way up in the air, about that high, / and he makes me try to climb
19	over it, / and then as soon as I get just about to the top of his feet, he
7	
5	tips me over. / and I fall down on the floor. / Sometimes it kind of hurts. /

_____

24 Units

112

Grade Seven   Age Twelve
(Looking at "The Gulf Stream," a Winslow Homer picture of a man adrift in the ocean)

13 9	I think this man went out just to have fun sailing one day, / and all of
8 4	the sudden a storm came up, / and it looks like he had a sail, / but it broke
21	off. / Now he's out in the middle of this water with the waves real high and
1-②-12 9	with sharks swimming around him, / and [he's] . . looks like he's looking for help
9	in back of the boat, / but up in front of him is a ship, / but I don't think
9 5	he has seen it. / Probably he will turn around and see the ship, / and then
7-①-5	signal for it. / There's also a tornado, I guess, [coming] coming at him
16	from behind, / and I think he will signal to this ship in front of him and get help. /

12 Units

Grade Twelve   Age Seventeen
(Telling about the book *The Jealous Man from Estremadura*)

25	Well, the one I would like to talk about is called *El Celoso Extremeño*
	which means *The Jealous Extremaduran*, I guess it is in English. / This is
2-①-11	[a] a jealous man who lives in a certain part of Spain. / He goes to Peru at
22	an early age in order to explore and seek his fortune like many Spaniards of
6	the day. / This is about the Sixteenth Century. / When he gets back twenty years
7-①-4 12	later [he] he's now rich, / and his only worry is that he doesn't have a
9 13	family. / There's an important point that comes up here. / When he gets back
6	his old friends don't like him any more; / they don't exactly hate him / but
24	they just don't associate with him so that he realizes that money doesn't
	bring him complete happiness when he gets back. / So what he decides to do is
30	to marry somebody and leave his money to a son or daugher so at least he'll
15	be of some good to somebody. / What he does then is he marries a girl who's
6 6	about thirteen years old, / and he's about sixty-eight / and it's kind of amazing, /
20	but since the parents of the girl knew he was a rich man, they allowed the girl
12	to marry him, / and the girl didn't have that much to say about it. /

16 Units

(Angelo's review of the book continues for several more transcribed pages of similar language.)

Written Composition

Grade Three   Age Eight

7	This picture looks like a boat sunk / and all the people are going
9	to the bottom. / The boat must have been an old fashioned one and must
16	have been close to land. /

3 Units

Grade Seven   Age Twelve

The Storm /

16	One day Mary, Jack, and Susan went fishing on a small rock island
8	in Andrews' Bay. / Only one fish was caught in the morning, / but Susan
8	found some interesting weeds and shells. /
15	While the children were eating a small lunch they had brought, it
7	began to rain. / Before long it became a raging storm. / Their small
9	boat was torn away from the rocks, / and the water almost covered the
8	entire island. /
	When the storm finally abated, the children were stranded for
20	three hours before they were rescued by the coast guard. /

8 Units

Grade Twelve   Age Seventeen

The Baffled Policeman /

15	Policeman are supposed to be strong, determined, and able to quickly
17	cope with any emergency. / They handle so many problems so well that some
	people get the idea that policemen are superhuman. / Nevertheless, even
7	police officers can become puzzled. /
17	One night Officer James Roberts, a motorcycle policeman, chased a
7	speeding car down a dark city street. / It was one o'clock in the
8	morning, / and there were few cars on the road. / Finally the speeding
8	driver pulled to a halt. / Officer Roberts stopped at the curb several
22	yards in front of the car and, pencil in hand, started walking toward
15	the vehicle. / Suddenly he noticed a pair of ladies' black flats in the

9	middle of the street. / Immediately a befuddled look appeared on the
	officer's face. /
21	The chain of events leading to the appearance of the black shoes
15	on the street had begun about four hours earlier. / A young lady, Mary
	Vincent, had bought the flats at an auction late that night. / Fortunately
27	they were a little too big, for when she was suddenly dragged into a car
	by a couple of kidnappers, the shoes remained on the street. / The crooks,
21	being in a hurry, did not stop to pick up the flats even after they
	noticed Mary's stocking feet. /
19	Officer Roberts stared at the shoes for some time before walking
13	over to the car and issuing a ticket. / After the car left, he studied
11	the situation for a few more minutes. / The strange thing was that the
10	shoes were in walking position. / It looked as if someone had disappeared
	into thin air. /
12	Within five minutes Officer Warren Strong brought Roberts out of
15	his trance. / Led by Strong, the city police force eventually saved
7	Mary Vincent from her hoodlum captors. / You can sometimes puzzle one
7	policeman, / but you can never baffle them all. /

22 Units

Barry L.
Random Group
Transcripts of Oral Language

Grade One   Age Six
(Looking at a Mardi Gras parade scene)

4/7	It's a circus / There's a clown and some puppets / and the clowns are playing
6	
7	something / There's a lady with a mask / There's a soldier / [There's a . . .]
4	
③-8	There's a wagon with men pulling it / and there's a lady with a flag / and there's
8	
8-①-2	a man on it playing [a] a horn / and then there's a man playing another horn /
9	
7	There is a thing that they wiggle.

10 Units

Grade Seven   Age Twelve
(Looking at "The Gulf Stream," a Winslow Homer picture of a man adrift in the ocean)

6	Well, see, there's this man / [he's marooned marooned on an island with all shark
(15½)-7	
8	——I mean he's remooned re-] Well, he's stuck on a boat / and all these
12	sharks are all around him / and there's this big tidal wave is coming up
8	over him / and he sees this boat on the horizon / and so he starts waving /
5	
7	but the boat doesn't see him / so the boat goes right by / but then [he fixes up
6	
2-⑧-5	the boat — for he can] he fixes up the motor / He has a little bit of gasoline
14	
6	left to get him to the boat / so he gets to the boat / and they bring him ashore /
5	
6	and he lives happily ever after. /

13 Units

Grade Twelve   Age Seventeen
(Telling about the book *Jim Taylor, Fullback*)

17	It's about Jim Taylor's life, his playing career, and all the great things he has
6	
②-11	done /. Well, he's a great fullback /. [and he] Next to Jimmy Brown, he's
8	
6-⑥-1-①-3	the best in the league /. I think he's better than Jimmy Brown / but most of the
5-①-4	papers say [he's just as he's] Jimmy [Brown] Brown's better / but all around
7	he's [just —] just a football player /. There is nothing else he can do /.
24	Because he works on weights every day, he can't even turn his neck because he's
18	just developed his neck muscles so much / but every time he carries the ball
6	he has a average of five point two yards to carry /. He scored fourteen touchdowns
8-②-5	last year / and I guess he's about the toughest [football uh fu-] fullback
④-7	in the National League /. [not that he's] He's about the smallest one, too /
5	
7	but he just has desire / and that's what keeps him going /.

14 Units

Written Composition

Grade Three   Age Eight

6/10	well the Bote gate gurt up / and all the pelpl are frill out of the bote / ther are
3/4	
5	forh / and there are crat / and the town nerd bey / and the Bote is the kote / and the
6	
5	mar are down. /

7 Units

(When Barry read his composition aloud, he read: Well, the boat got hurt up / and all the people are falling out of the boat / . There are fish / and there are crabs / and the town near by / and the boat is the hole / and the men are down.)

Grade Seven Age Twelve

17	As Tom the boy the biggest was casting his line he got it cough in John skin. /
9	
7	John was crying, but finly we got it out. / So we went back agin the casting. /
11	
5	But this time I was lucky, when I cated the line. / it didn't get cought. / moreovery
6	
12	it went in the water. / But then it happened the river started to get higer and
15	higer. / Tom went and grab John shirttale, and Mary pigtall. And got them out
13	in time. / In the very same spot where they were fishing it was under water. /
10	
6	All the fish they left on the rock were gone. / So they got no fish dinner. /

11 Units

Grade Twelve Age Seventeen

	Walking down the street one rainy saturday night we came upon a
28	piculier sight a policeman giving a ticket to a woman who had jaywalked
7	accross the street. / What a heated argument was going on, / the woman whom
16	I had never seen before was trying to convince the policeman of something, /
10	We could not make out exactly what they were saying, / so curious as were are,
14	we crept up closer & closer. Step by step / finally we could hear every
10	word that they were saying. / She keep telling to policeman I had to
9	
11	jaywalk / I thought I saw my sons rain boots in the street, / there's no
10	robbers in the middle of the street. / Even though the cop did see the
31	slippers behind the woman he could not change his mind for he needed
	the 10% commission he would obtain from that sort of violation. / So he
24	gave her the ticket but found out latter she was dective mores from the
	state police which conjured up the whole situation. /

11 Units

Boyd R.
Low Proficiency Group
Transcripts of Oral Language

Grade One   Age Six
(After mentioning a ride on a train, Boyd was asked if anything funny happened.)

5 1-①-5	Nothing funny happened to me. . / . but [I] I only seen things funny. /
3	Cartoons are funny. / On one cartoon . . you know there was a tractor
10 12	there, / and the tractor lifted up some little animal that were on it. /
3 5	That was funny. / And do you know what? / That tractor was a steam roller /
6 ⑤-2-①-5 8	[an an an the shu] and a [shov] shovel was on the steamroller. . . . /
5 5	I could tell you one about this picture. / I could really tell you. / It looks
①-8 12	like a circus. / [An] And there's a big clown right there, / and there's a
3-③-5 8	man coming out of the clown right there. / Clown's holding [a man on] two mans
7 9	on its head / It's a wagon that he's in / That was the end of that one /
10 6	They're playing and having a lot of fun. / They are here because of that big
8	man right there. / He's sitting down on something, / but I don't know what it is /

21 Units

Grade Seven   Age Twelve
(Telling about the book he liked best during the year)

12 10 8	Well I'll tell you about Tom Swift and the Flying Lab / well at the beginning there were these spies from Mexico / and they were trying to
5-③-3	find some uranium / and so they came into [this this was] Tom Swift's plant /
9-①-8 8	and they hit his son over the head with [his] his gun well with the back
①-24	of it / and then they were trying to find him / [they] and there was this other man from Mexico would ask him if he asked Mr. Swift if he would like
8 1-②½-11 9	to join his club / I forget what the name of it was / and [uh, uh, um he] he got up and was on the stage at the club / and he was telling the people
8-②-5	about him himself / and then they saw this man that clobbered [his well] his son
6 ⑤½-2-①- 5-②-3 12	over the head / and his son went after him / [and so uh and then the] and then [they] his son was flying around [in a] in his jet / and he found this landing
1-⑥½-5	field that he didn't know about / and [uh] then he decided to land / and when
4-②-7- ②-18	he landed [there was] there was this same man that had [uh that cap] captured him kind of and tied him up and put him inside the shack that was near by /

16 Units

Grade Twelve   Age Seventeen
(Reaction to a statement on the irresponsibility of children and parents)

4-⑫-6-⑫-10	Well from the first [uh] sentence where it says younger generation [ir]
9	wild and irresponsible I don't think that's true / and why I don't think
6	it's true? / well sure they do wild things / but it's no different like
13	our parents did when they were kids / and it says farther down here fathers
16	are too busy to pay attention to their children / I don't think any father's
15 ③-6 9	too busy to pay attention to his kids / [I mean he] well he might be too busy /
6	but he could always find time for his kids / at least I feel that way /
1-⑫-14-⑫-10	and [uh] to say that as a result kids grow up to be rather childish and
1-⑫-5-⑫-6- ⑤-7	[uh] irresponsible but I don't think that's true either / and [uh] another part
	of it say [uh] it's the parents' fault and [why kids are always getting] why
	kids are the way they are / I don't think that it's the parents' fault
29	because the kids have modern ideas and because the parents have ideas
⑩	that they had when they were young / [so I don't think it's of it's] / it's
7	probably a combination of both / but I don't really think that it's anybody's
16	fault the way the kids act.

14 Units

Written Composition

Grade Three   Age Eight

8 5 8 9 8	It lookeses liked a boat is tip over / and piple our swimy out / And it lookies liked a man is ded. / And the men our tring to get on land / And some fich our looking up at them. /

5 Units

Grade Seven   Age Twelve

8 4 6 12 8	It looks to me that they are fishing / and ther our camping. / The Boy Just cast out his line. / The girl has had here line in the water fore a while / and the other girl is bating hir line. /
15	Afture theyr fished for a while they will take the fish home for dinner. /

6 Units

Grade Twelve   Age Seventeen

15   A few nights ago this girl (Serca) was in town staying with her

23   girl friend. / They decided to take a pair of there old shoes and put

them in the street so that it might create some publicity. / So that

26   night they were driving back from the show and left the shoes in the

middle of the street and then went home to bed. / Later that night a

15   policeman came bay and saw the shoes and wrote a report. / The next day

19   the girls looked in the paper and sure enough there was a picture of their *shoes*. /

5 Units

APPENDIX E

PRACTICAL EVALUATION OF ORAL LANGUAGE

Until spoken English is evaluated in education, oral language will continue to be neglected to the detriment of all the language arts. The curriculum inevitably shrinks to the boundaries of whatever evaluation the schools use. At present, an inadequate understanding of the highly limited scope of paper and pencil standardized tests in English results in a narrow, warped curriculum. What is easy to measure is not necessarily what is important to evaluate, and most tests measure a shockingly narrow range of what should be evaluated. The result is that curriculum decisions are made upon this meager basis.

Eventually the evaluation of oral language will require tape recorders and cassettes, and the features of language to be evaluated will be variables such as organization showing sensitivity to the listener, liveliness and vitality of speech, and freedom from distracting speech mannerisms. Because this kind of evaluation is time-consuming, schools may need to select random samples for evaluation; a teacher or a school system will attain a picture of a class of thirty pupils by using a random sample of ten or eleven pupils. For the present, teachers need some relatively simple way of estimating growth in language power.

One way of overcoming the time-consuming barrier to evaluation might be to examine some of the oral language variables in the present research. Could any one of the variables serve to represent other variables? Mazes and conventionality of speech, for instance, are logically quite unlike other variables; however, length of communication unit, elaboration of subject and predicate, and use of dependent clauses may be similar enough to simplify the problem of evaluation.

As one can easily observe by examining our data, oral dependent clause measures are highly correlated with oral elaboration measures as well as with length of oral communication units. At grades one, two, and three, the values of the correlations are given by $r_{EC} = .80$ and $r_{ED} = .82$. Here, E stands for Elaboration of subject and predicate; C stands for length of communication unit (average number of words per communication unit); D stands for

Dependent clause measures (average number of dependent clauses per communication unit). These high correlations make sense, of course, because elaboration of simple subject and predicate in the units of communication increases the length of the units and the incidence of dependent clauses. However, inasmuch as the measurement of elaboration is complex and time-consuming, even though it is the best indicator of language power in our research, it is reasonable to speculate as to whether or not elaboration could be predicted with any reliability from the more easily determined communication unit length and a measure of dependent clauses. To determine whether such a prediction possesses an acceptable level of reliability, a multiple regression analysis was carried out on the elaboration index at grades one, two, and three, combined with communication unit length and number of dependent clauses as the predicter variables. The results of this analysis are summarized in Table 1.

Table 1

Multiple Regression Analysis
Analysis of Elaboration Index on Average Number of Words per Communication Unit
and Number of Dependent Clauses Measured

Variable	Regression Coefficient	t-value	Decision*
Average words per communication unit	.41	10.9	Significant
Dependent Clauses	.53	12.4	Significant

*Significant at $\leq$ .05.

According to this analysis, the prediction is definitely reliable. The multiple correlation coefficient is given by $R_{E.CD}$ + .89 with the prediction equation given by

$$E + 3.00 + 41C + .53D.$$

The standard error for the estimated elaboration index is given by SE = 3.72. On the basis of these results, Table 2 has been prepared. From this table a researcher or a teacher can estimate a primary school pupil's elaboration index score from the average number of words per communication unit and the average number of dependent clauses per communication unit. Also, the 95% confidence interval for the true elaboration index score can be determined by adding and subtracting seven points from the predicted value. For example, if $T_C = 40$ and $T_D = 60$, then the predicted elaboration index score is given $T_E = 51 \pm 7$. As another example, suppose $T_C = 34$ and $T_D = 58$. To estimate the elaboration index, use $T_C = 49 \pm 7$. In other words, use the closest values in Table 4 when T_C or T_D fall between the intervals provided there.

Thus it is important, both for research and for classroom evaluation of oral language, to know that in grades one, two, and three a count of the two elements,

- length of communication unit (average number of words per communication unit)

- average number of dependent clauses per communication unit

Table 2

Predicted Elaboration Index Standardized Value from Observed Standardized Communication Unit and Dependent Clause Scores

Standardized Dependent Clause Score	*Standardized Communication Unit Score**								
	30	35	40	45	50	55	60	65	70
30	31	33	35	37	39	42	44	46	48
35	34	36	38	40	42	44	46	48	50
40	37	39	41	43	45	47	49	51	53
45	39	41	44	46	48	50	52	54	56
50	42	44	46	48	50	52	54	56	58
55	44	46	48	50	52	54	56	58	60
60	47	49	51	53	55	57	59	61	64
65	50	51	54	56	58	60	62	64	66
70	52	54	57	59	61	63	65	67	69

*Standardized scores for average number of words per communication unit and for dependent clauses were computed by assigning the numeral 50 to their means and the numeral 10 to one standard deviation from the mean:

$$T_E = \frac{T_{E1} + T_{E2} + T_{E3}}{3} = 50 + 10 \left\{ \frac{1}{3} \left[\frac{X_{E1} - 75.4 + X_{E2} - 81.6 + X_{E3} - 89.4}{27.6 \quad\quad 24.8 \quad\quad 27.4} \right] \right\}$$

$$T_C = 50 + 10 \left\{ \frac{1}{3} \left[\frac{X_{C1} - 6.0 + X_{C2} - 6.5 + X_{C3} - 6.9}{1.39 \quad\quad 1.38 \quad\quad 1.32} \right] \right\}$$

$$T_D = 50 + 10 \left\{ \frac{1}{3} \left[\frac{X_{D1} - .07 + X_{D2} - .07 + X_{D3} - .06}{.04 \quad\quad 0.4 \quad\quad 0.4} \right] \right\}$$

will serve almost as effectively as a count of all three language variables. Thus the time-consuming and complex computation of the elaboration index including all syntactic devices (such as infinitive clauses, appositives, gerunds, adjectives, etc.) may be bypassed, yet the valuable index score can nevertheless be ascertained. A similar multiple regression analysis could be performed for the upper elementary grades, junior high, and senior high school. This simplification can be tried also for written language at any point of schooling. Schools will want their own norms for all of these measures, of course.

One of our analysts was troubled at the amount of time we had spent on studying the elaboration of subject and predicate, but eventually she came to see that the effort enabled us to validate the use of simpler measures such as average length (in words) of the communication unit.

If we were to apply this to a practical situation in a school district we would make these recommendations, assuming that time and money were not in great supply:

> For oral language, the three elements we would study would be average number of words per communication unit, vocabulary, and expressive intonation. We would tape pupils' oral language in some natural but standard situation, such as telling a story from one of the books that presents a story in pictures but uses no words. From that tape we would distill the length of communication unit and the depth of vocabulary. (One might, in addition, use some vocabulary test in which the teachers had faith. For small children we found the Watts Vocabulary test to be sound.)

> We consider expressive intonation to be exceptionally important for it shows whether or not the pupil is learning to be aware of listeners, to put him/herself in the shoes of the audience. To measure this we would prepare three adults to listen independently to the tapes, not knowing the age or names of the pupils speaking. They would simply rate the pupil as superior, average, or weak in the kind of expressiveness— pitch, stress, pause, and rhythm—that aids communication of ideas.

If taping all the pupils in a class proved too time-consuming or expensive, a school could easily take a random sample of every fifth child, and base its evaluation on that sample.

We have had in mind here early childhood education and the primary grades, but adaptation to upper grades and high school is entirely possible. Evaluation such as we have described, accomplished in September, February, and May, would give schools much better evidence on pupil growth in language than they now have with paper and pencil tests, so dangerous in their narrowness.

APPENDIX F

TRANSFORMATIONAL SYNTAX: A DESIGN FOR ANALYSIS
by John Dennis

In devising the categories of syntactic oral performance of students, I have been guided—or constrained—by the following evidence and studies:

- four sets of protocols of the actual language used by selected students, each set consisting of approximately eighteen communication units (Loban) or T-units (Hunt)[1]
- the Bateman and Zidonis monograph, "The Transformational Model of Generative or Predictive Grammar" by Robert Stockwell, and Roberts' *Modern Grammar*.[2]

Naturally, there is overlapping and contradiction among the studies. I have tried to find areas of agreement when they exist in some form; further, I have tried to reduce the number of transform "types" in order to avoid unreal or unnecessarily complex descriptions. My guide for theoretical decisions was the corpus of oral protocols provided me.

Of course the corpus under study really strains the resources of a "one-sentence grammar," no matter how much descriptive adequacy we attribute to that grammar. I say this because this present corpus is discursive living language with all the natural language features we have come to expect of such material: rhetorical strategies in evidence, a high degree of recursiveness in structures, shifts in topic and register (level of "appropriate usage"), hesitation phenomena, some deviations from rigidly described well-formed sentences, etc. Consequently, I have attempted to devise a description ignoring evident rhetorical concerns and focusing instead on syntactic performance. At this point I will present categories, descriptions, and justifications.

Single-Base Transforms

So far as I know, all single-base transforms involve two kinds of structural operations: (1) reordering of constituents in statements, and (2) insertion of optional incremental elements *not* derived from other statements. *Statement* here refers to what we have come to call "kernel" sentences, which are characterized by the following criteria: they are statements; they are positive; they are active. We used to say that they were "irreducible," but in saying this, we were at a loss to explain items and phrases used adverbially. Since it is clearly simpler and sounder to consider words like *there*, *then*, and *thus* and their phrasal equivalents as aspects of phrase structure, (2) makes sense as an option available to kernels. A similar procedure must be followed in making incremental (wh-) questions; interrogatives like *what, who(m), when,* and *where* are simply optional attachments to the reorder or intonational shift underlying this type of (wh-) question. The same argument applies to negation expressed by not + lexical verb.

1) T neg: NP + Aux + be + not + $\begin{pmatrix} NP \\ Adj \\ Adv \end{pmatrix}$; NP + Aux + not + V ± NP

2) T there: There + Aux + be + NP ± $\begin{pmatrix} Adv \\ V\text{-ing} \end{pmatrix}$

3) T yes/no: Aux + be + NP + $\begin{pmatrix} NP \\ Adj \\ Adv \end{pmatrix}$; Do + tense + NP + V ± NP

4) T wh- $\begin{pmatrix} what \\ when \\ where \end{pmatrix}$ + tense + do + NP + V (± Np); Who + tense + V ± Np

5) T passive: NP_1 + Aux + V_{tr} + NP_2 ⬧ NP_2 + tense + be + part +

   V + by + NP_1

6) T mobility: NP + Aux + V ± NP + Prep Phr ⬧ Prep Phr + S —

I don't think we need to list citations illustrating these structural descriptions at this time. In this report we will do what Bateman and Zidonis have done, avoiding scrupulously the term transformational *rules*. They aren't rules at all; they are *types* of *optional* transforms.

Multi-Base Transforms

When *two or more single bases*—kernels or their transforms— are used to make grammatical sequences of complex types, we can refer to them as multi-base transforms, thus avoiding the tiresome enumeration problem (double-base, triple-base, etc.) An alternative way of describing the derivations resulting from various choices and subsequent manipulations is *matrix/insert* operations. Such a description makes good sense within the limits of a "one-sentence grammar," where constraints on the length and complexity of sentences used for analysis are likely. However, in the analysis of a discourse sample, a multiplicity of matrices and inserts is probable; consequently, there is a problem in description which can be avoided if we stick to a description of the structural manipulations performed. There doesn't seem to be a compelling reason for a *double* entry: e.g., *The boy whom he saw at the game was his neighbor.* This is a "double-base" (multi-base) transform using T_{sub} (subordination). Its basic sentences are evident, and its transformational history is obvious. *Whom he saw at the game* is an *insert* sentence, surrounded by the *matrix, The boy . . . was his neighbor.* It seems unnecessary to point out that when bases are combined they are either embedded or conjoined, with or without deletions.

Another feature of sentence analysis which I consider unnecessary—unless, of course, a highly detailed description of a "notional" kind is the analyst's aim—is the use of functional labels like "That + sentence as subject," "nominal infinitive of obligation," "abstractive nominal," "adverbial expansion of Man (adverb of manner) + C" (presumably "complement," that catch-all term). First of all, what do these labels tell us? How are they "transformational rules"? Are they more or less accurate than descriptions of transformational types which are manipulated to produce grammatical sequences? These labels tell *me* that someone is trying to explain optional transformations in terms of traditional-school grammar. Chomsky spends a good deal of patient argument in *Aspects of the Theory of Syntax* to discount the value of mixing functional labels with grammatical categories.[3]

I will sum up my argument this way: If we are interested in developing a "syntactic profile" of a given student, student group, or "level" in school, we can surely obtain that information without recourse to matrix/insert counts or notional labels. For example, recurrent syntactic structures could be generalized *abstractly* this way: This student/group/grade tends to conjoin more frequently than he or she/it tends to embed. More specifically we could say that conjoining structures were used 57% of the time in all units analyzed; *and, but,* and *or* were so used in relative order of frequency. Suppose the reverse were true; then we could specify the types of embedded transforms: relative, subordinate, appositive, etc., depending on how we specified deletion.

Multi-Base Transforms (Full Forms)

The term *full form* means that the entire transformation is intact; there has been no deletion.

$$
\left\{
\begin{array}{l}
1)\ \text{T conj. } S_1 \begin{pmatrix} (\text{and}) \\ (\text{but }) \\ (\text{or }) \end{pmatrix} S_2;\ IC_1 \begin{pmatrix} (\text{and}) \\ (\text{but }) \\ (\text{or }) \end{pmatrix} IC_2 \\
\quad\quad .\,.\,.\,. \\
\\
2)\ \text{T con(nector) } S_1 \begin{pmatrix} (\text{therefore }) \\ (\text{however }) \\ (\text{consequently}) \end{pmatrix} S_2 \\
\quad\quad\quad .\,.\,.\,.
\end{array}
\right.
$$

3) T rel(ative) $\left[S_1 \begin{pmatrix} (\text{who }) \\ (\text{which}) \\ (\text{that }) \\ (\text{whose}) \end{pmatrix} + \text{Aux} + \text{VP} \ldots \right]$

$$
\left\{
\begin{array}{l}
4)\ \text{T sub(ordinate) } \left[S_1\ (+\ \text{sub} + S_2) \ldots \right] \\
\\
5)\ \text{T pro (It + Aux + be + Adj + sub + S \ldots)} \\
\quad\quad\quad\ (\text{I\ \ + Aux + be + Adj + sub + S \ldots})
\end{array}
\right.
$$

6) T for-to* For + NP + to + V + VP . . .
          * #5 often combines here: It + Aux + be + Adj +
                                 for + NP + to + VP

7) T to NP + Aux + V_{tr} + NP + S_2

    ◆John wanted *NP + John* + tense + come
    ◆John wanted ϕ + to   + come

8) T nom NP + $\begin{pmatrix} (V_{intr}) \\ (V_{tr}) \end{pmatrix}$ ± NP / NP + be + $\begin{pmatrix} (\text{Adj}) \\ (\text{Adv}) \end{pmatrix}$ ◆

    NP + grow   / NP is interesting ◆
    NP + grow + NP

    also *The* growing of flowers is interesting
      — flying — kites can be troublesome

9) T comp NP + V_{tr} + *comp.* + VP ◆

    They consider he is foolish him ◆
    They consider him (to be) foolish

10) T mob(ility) I like him because he is honest ◆

    Because he is honest I like him
    (Many other examples are possible here.)[4]

It is apparent to those of us who have examined the natural uses of language that deletion of certain items and structures is commonplace in both speech and writing. Deletion is often treated as a transform, a *single* type of generalized option. In a way that's sensible, but I don't think we've treated it systematically enough. Deletion is like the *recursive rule*: it can be applied indefinitely to certain strings in a given environment; and so long as the specifications are correctly followed, grammatical sequences will result.

To sum up, then, we should be interested in the subject's uses of the various kinds of deletions as he applies them to items and structures in the sentences he generates.

1) D NP $NP_1 + VP_1 + conj + NP_1 + VP_2$ ▶$NP_1 + VP_1 + \phi + VP_2$ ▶
   [env. T conj]
                   Mr. Smith bent over and tied his shoelace.

2) D rel + Aux   The man who is sick ▶ The man sick ▶ The sick man
   [env. T rel]   The girl who is crying ▶ The girl crying ▶
                      The crying girl
                   The man who is smoking ▶ The man smoking -----

   Note 1: The same operation applies to strings which have undergone the *pas-sive* - T passive:
                   The man who was injured ▶ The man injured -----
                   The man who was frightened ▶ The man frightened ▶
                      The frightened man.

   Note 2: There is an *inversion rule* operative here, but it applies with consis-tency only to "attributives." With -*ing* forms, there is divided usage.

   Note 3: This D rule also accounts for the *appositive*.

3) D NP + V   The class elected *comp.* John ▶
   [env. T comp]   The class elected John became president John
                   The class elected ϕ ϕ president John
                   (An inversion rule is *obligatory* here.)

4) D NP + for   For NP to solve the problem + VP
   [env. T for-to] ϕ ϕ to solve the problem is easy.

5) D sub.   The man whom I saw . . . ▶
   [env. T sub]   The man ϕ I saw

   Note: Only the "relatives," *who, which* and *that,* can be deleted in T sub; *whose* must be used, and the other subordinators are also obligatory.

6) D conj   This is obvious and will lead to a series of NPs,
   [env. T cong-and] attributes, verbs, etc.

7) D VP   I am taller than he is tall ▶
   [env. T compar.] I am taller than he is ϕ
                   ^{or}I am taller than he ϕ ϕ

   Note: I did not list *T compar.* with multi-base "full forms" because it is never a full form except in such oddities as *He is as handsome as she is ugly—* which *doesn't* strike me as a comparison, but rather as a variant form of the *contrast: He is handsome but she is ugly*.

8) D V   I enjoy chess, and John enjoys chess (too)
   [env. T conj.] I enjoy chess, and John ϕ does too
                   I enjoy chess, and so does John.

Performance Deviations

We can take care of the various deviations in performance under three rubrics: (1) mazes; (2) sequence interrupters and parenthetical structures; (3) syntactic deviations. Two of these can in the sense of *hesitation phenomena* be called deviations of some kind. The third is well known.

1. *Mazes*: I should think that two kinds of evidence might be useful here.

   a. Kinds of maze structures = item, phrase, clause
   b. Movement = complete break-off (aposiopesis) or stop-and-revision (anacoluthon).

2. *Sequence Interrupters and Parenthetical Structures*

   a. Sequence Interrupters: I think of these as *non-initial*. When they are initial (before communication units), they tend to move the discourse along. When they are *internal*, they usually represent a pause for decision-making. Their *position* interests me, too, and I would chart them thus:

Type	*Position*
uh	NP: medial/terminal
um	VP: medial/terminal
well	Inter-sentence
. . . .	

   b. Parenthetical Structures:
   (1) S + deletion: let's see
                   you see
                   you know
                   I would think
                   you might say
                   as it were
   (2) frozen items and phrases: as a matter of fact
                                    for that matter
                                    of course
                                    in other words
                                    generally speaking
                                    in my opinion

3. *Syntactic Deviations*

   a. Non-sentences
   b. Word order: items or structures out of sequence
   c. Number: non-agreement on NP + VP
                   pronoun reference: $NP_{sing} \blacktriangleright Pro_{pl}$

    d. Preposition or particle: to ▶ on
                      with ▶ to
    e. Deletions: article omitted; connective omitted, etc.
    f. Tense shift: narrative past ▶ narrative present
                He went ▶ He goes . . .
    g. Other: (one always needs an *etc.*)

In offering here a sketch and suggestions for procedures, I think the analyst could mark the protocols, using brackets to enclose the segments of language he is classifying, and labeling the bracketed material so he can make a quick tally of transformational types after finishing his analysis. Let me present a typical problem. Suppose a student has used *T passive*, then *T relative*, and finally *D Rel + Aux*. How would the analyst judge and mark this material? I would say that the *final* structure would be coded—i.e., *D rel + Aux* because this "result" implies the underlying transformational history. Thus the past participle used as a modifier and so specified by *D rel + Aux* reveals a *hierarchy* of manipulative skills as a review of its transformational history confirms. I think that this procedure plus judgment will stand up under scrutiny in most cases. It's rather a novel idea, and I encourage inquiry. In any case, I fail to see that the *entire* transformational history I've just described could be coded without giving a curious imbalance to the syntactic profile we wish to obtain.

Unless there is a desire to see what a given student has done *within* any specific communication unit, I see no reason for describing the *locus* of optional transforms as unit 1, unit 6, etc. I think that one page of code symbols for one set of protocols (30 T-units) would be sufficient. However, a master tally sheet for a student, a student group, or a "level" of instruction (or achievement) would probably have to be more complex.

Of course, in this proposal I know I have not said all that needs to be said about the scheme for analysis and description of the optional transforms students use in casual discourse. However, I do believe that I have presented enough to make an accurate and productive analysis possible.

APPENDIX G

INTERVIEW FOR GRADES KINDERGARTEN THROUGH THREE

In order to parallel the increasing maturity of the subjects, the questions and pictures were changed for grades 4-6, for grades 7-9, and for grades 10-12. Many inquiries have been received concerning the possibility of using our pictures. We feel that any well-chosen pictures will produce the same results. Researchers should find pictures that are relatively complex and ambiguous; such pictures seem to elicit more language. If we were to do this research again, we would use a few sets (of four to six pictures) which would suggest a sequence of events. However, we would still retain some of our single pictures such as the complex Mardi Gras scene.

Opening questions:

1. First of all, tell me your whole name.
2. When you are at home, who do you play with?
3. What do you and [Names of playmates] do when you are at home?
   (Pretend ignorance of games, etc., and get the child to explain how they play these games.)
4. Do you like television? What programs do you like best? Tell me all about them. (Often, the child will tell about just one program.)
5. Have you ever been sick? Tell me about that.
6. What do you like to do best of everything in the whole world?

Pictures:

Now I am going to show you some pictures, and I want you to tell me all about the pictures. Will you do that? I want you to tell me everything you see in the pictures and what you think about the pictures. (If the child's first response to the picture itself covers the area of one of the subquestions, omit the subquestion.)

1. This is picture number one. (Boy holding cocker spaniel puppy; girl bandaging paw.) What can you tell me about this picture?

2. This is picture number two. (In color, Mardi Gras scene.) Will you tell me all about this picture?

   a. What can you tell me about all these?
   b. What are they doing?
   c. Why do you think they are all here?

3. This is picture number three. (Two Korean girls, the older one crying.) What can you tell me about this picture?

   a. Where do you think these children are?
   b. Which one would you like for a playmate? (If the child points, say, "The one on the right," or "The one on the left.")
   c. Why did you choose that one? (If the child says "Because," say, "Because why?" If the child should state that these children are Oriental or Mexican or some other designation, ask "How do you know they are Oriental?" (or Mexican, etc.)

4. This is picture number four. (Northern lights, snow, dog sled.) Will you tell me all about this picture?

   a. What are they doing? (In case the child notices sled, etc.)
   b. Where do you think they are going? (In case the child notices driver, dogs, etc.)
   c. What is this? (Do *not* say "Up in the sky." Point to the lights, even if the child does not notice the Northern lights.)

5. This is picture number five. (Small boy running and crying, a dog, two small girls watching him, part of a woman in the picture.) Will you tell me all about this picture?

   a. Why do you think he is crying? (If child says boy is crying.)
   b. Can you tell me a story about this picture? Can you pretend a story?

6. This is picture number six. (Small girl picking up a rabbit, dark photographic background.) Tell me all about this picture, will you?[1]

NOTES TO CHAPTER ONE

1. Walter Loban, *The Language of Elementary School Children; Language Ability: Grades Seven, Eight, and Nine; Problems in Oral English;* Walter Loban and Leonard A. Marascuilo, *An Empirical Study of the Dominating Predictive Features of Spoken Language: A Multivariate Description and Analysis of Oral Language Development* (Washington, D. C.: Office of Education, Department of Health, Education and Welfare, Project No. 7-1-106, 1969).

2. The initial method of determining spread of intellectual ability was a kindergarten vocabulary test of 100 items. In grade two the first standard intelligence testing was carried out by the Oakland Public Schools.

3. Annual ratings in which the thirteen or more teachers rated each subject's ability in language in accordance with a carefully designed scale. See page 5 for a description of this scale and Appendix A for a copy of the complete scale.

NOTES TO CHAPTER TWO

1. A. F. Watts, *The Language and Mental Development of Children*, pp. 65-66.

2. Some linguists object to any use of "communication" or "meaning," urging a rigorous use of structure alone. This investigator, however, has seen no problem in using meaning as a double-check on the structural methodology actually being used; some mistakes have been located in this way, no dilemmas have arisen, and the research has retained a closer alliance with the ultimate communicative purpose of language. Still another double check, occasionally used, has been that of verbal signalling—pitch, pause, and stress. One of our analysts defined the communication unit as "each independent clause, with all of its modifiers, existing between two silences." However, very few utterances were sufficiently ambiguous to force us into meticulous intonation analysis as a supplement to our usual methods.

3. Kellogg W. Hunt, *Grammatical Structures Written at Three Grade Levels.*

4. Other researchers have studied this same phenomenon although, again, there has been no consistency in terminology. Hunt, in *Grammatical Structures*, uses the term *garbles* rather than *mazes*. Others use *hesitation phenomena* (see Howard Maclay and Charles E. Osgood, "Hesitation Phenomena in Spontaneous English Speech," in *Readings in the Psychology of Language*, ed. Leon Jakobovits and Murray Miron [Englewood Cliffs, New Jersey: Prentice-Hall, 1967]).

5. In LaBrant's research a subordinate clause which modifies an independent element of the communication unit is termed "first-order subordination." Subordination which modifies another subordinate element, which in turn modifies an independent element, is called "second-order subordination." Lou LaBrant, "A Study of Certain Language Developments of Children in Grades Four to Twelve, Inclusive," *Genetic Psychology Monographs* 14 (1933): 387-491.

6. Mata V. Bear, "Children's Growth in the Use of Written Language," *Elementary English Review* 16 (1939): 312-319; F. K. Heider and G. M. Heider, "A Comparison of Sentence Structure of Deaf and Hearing Children," *Psychological Monographs* 52 (1940): 42-103.

7. Hunt, *Grammatical Structures*.

8. Mildred C. Templin, *Certain Language Skills in Children*, Child Welfare Monograph Series No. 26 (Minneapolis: University of Minnesota Press, 1957).

9. Roy C. O'Donnell, William J. Griffin, and Raymond C. Norris, *Syntax of Kindergarten and Elementary School Children*, p. 60. O'Donnell et al. found a different result for adjective clauses. They acknowledge that their result does not conform to the findings of others. Further study of the adjective clause is needed to sharpen and stabilize our knowledge of this kind of noun modification.

10. Denis Lawton, "Social Class Differences in Language Development: A Study of Some Samples of Written Work," *Language and Speech* 6 (1963): 120-43.

11. Walter Loban, *The Language of Elementary School Children*.

12. Lawton, "Social Class Differences in Language Development," p. 138.

13. For oral language alone the research includes 37,800 separate data sheets, each containing a wealth of information subject to analysis.

14. A tally was made to determine the actual incidence of each elaborated structure (appositive, modal, gerund, dependent clause, etc.); the most commonly used structures were accorded the least weight and the least commonly used structures the greatest weight.

15. Anthony L. Endicott, "A Proposed Scale for Syntactic Density," *Research in the Teaching of English* 7 (1973): 5-12.

16. Lester S. Golub and Carole Kidder, "Syntactic Density and the Computer," *Elementary English* 51 (1974): 1128-31.

17. Roy C. O'Donnell, "A Critique of Some Indices of Syntactic Maturity," *Research in the Teaching of English* 10 (1976): 31-38.

18. To be sure, there may be occasions when an awareness of the listener's (or reader's) needs will indicate a use of grammatical redundancy.

19. Don P. Brown, Thomas D. Kowalski, Bernard R. Tanner, and Melvin E. Tuohey, *Writing: Unit-Lessons in Composition*, Chapter IIc, Unit 12, "Increase Verb Density" (New York: Ginn and Company, 1964), p. 51. In the present research the investigator counted *every verb word* individually. For example, *can serve* is counted as two verb words; *is to furnish* is counted as two verb words (omitting the *to*); *will have served* is counted as three verb words; *would have liked to furnish* is counted as four verb words.

20. Robert L. Allen, *The Verb System of Present-Day American English*.

21. All verbs used in the thirty selected units of communication were identified, recorded on individual tally sheets, and then statistically tabulated.

NOTES TO CHAPTER THREE

1. In the investigation the socioeconomic ratings were carried out by two judges, and in cases of disagreement (which were actually negligible) the investigator himself provided a third judgment.

2. *The Minnesota Scale* contains approximately 500 occupations rated on a seven-point scale. It was developed at the Institute of

Child Welfare, University of Minnesota, as a basis for classifying persons into socioeconomic groups at a time when the Institute was looking for an instrument which would enable it to secure a cross section of the population. (See *The Minnesota Scale for Paternal Occupations* [Minneapolis: University of Minnesota Press, n.d.]).

3. Typically a socioeconomic rating of IV was the result of a mother who was a skilled clerical worker (III) and a father who was a semiskilled factory worker (V), resulting in an average of IV as the family socioeconomic rating.

NOTES TO CHAPTER FOUR

1. Walter Loban, *The Language of Elementary School Children*, p. 41.

2. Ibid., p. 78.

3. Ibid., p. 54.

4. In the case of *mazes*, no written data are presented since mazes as such do not occur in the subjects' written language. Even a poor writer does not *write* as follows: "There was was a was there was a man." A speaker may use such mazes, however. Some mixed-up language occurs—rather rarely—in writing; Hunt and O'Hare use the term *garbles* for such undecipherable writing.

5. See Frank O'Hare, *Sentence Combining*, p. 22 (Table 1) and p. 53 (Table 3) for comparisons.

6. The investigator has termed the overlapping a quirk since it is apparent that it is explained by a downward shift by the Random group rather than an upward shift by the Low group.

7. James Moffett, "Grammar and the Sentence," in *Teaching the Universe of Discourse* (Boston: Houghton-Mifflin, 1968).

8. The reader should keep in mind that the growth rate percentages simply place the data in better perspective. The identical conclusion could be drawn from the averages themselves (the first column in Table 8) or from the graphic presentation of the averages (Figure 5). In other words, one could just as easily have said that the High group average of 0.37 at grade four was not achieved by the Low group until grade eleven (0.36).

9. The data, reported in a different publication, show the very clear superiority of the High group. (See Walter Loban, *Language Ability: Grades Ten, Eleven, and Twelve*.)

10. This computation is *not* a measure of average number of words *per* dependent clause. In any given communication unit, a subject may use no dependent clauses whatsoever or as many as three or four dependent clauses *within* that single unit, resulting in a mathematical tendency for the average words *per* dependent clause to decline in cases where there is more than one dependent clause within the unit. For this reason it was decided that the best measure would be words in dependent clauses as a percentage of words in units.

11. Kellogg W. Hunt, *Grammatical Structures Written at Three Grade Levels*; A. F. Watts, *The Language and Mental Development of Children*, p. 125.

12. Because of the inconclusive nature of the findings on written language, this breakdown of the data will be presented *only* for the subjects' oral language.

13. Denis Lawton, "Social Class Differences in Language Development: A Study of Some Samples of Written Work," *Language and Speech* 6 (1963): 120-24.

14. Hunt, *Grammatical Structures*; Roy C. O'Donnell, William J. Griffin, and Raymond C. Norris, *Syntax of Kindergarten and Elementary School Children*; Donald R. Bateman and Frank J. Zidonis, *The Effect of a Study of Transformational Grammar on the Writing of Ninth and Tenth Graders.* Research Report No. 6 (Urbana, Ill.: National Council of Teachers of English, 1966).

15. Another most commonly used adverbial clause, in addition to *time* and *cause*, is *condition*; percentages for these three are high for *all* groups.

16. Kellogg W. Hunt, "Recent Measures in Syntactic Development," *Elementary English* 43 (1966): 734.

17. Lou LaBrant, "A Study of Certain Language Developments of Children in Grades Four to Twelve, Inclusive," *Genetic Psychology Monographs* 14 (1933): 387-491.

18. See Appendix E for further discussion of practical application of research to school evaluation of language growth.

19. For readers unfamiliar with the terminology of transformational grammar, an example of multi-base deletion transformations could be the following transforming (combining) kernel sentences with deletion of words no longer needed:
I know a boy, and he has red hair, and he has a rabbit. It is his pet.
I know a red-haired boy who has a pet rabbit.

Further discussion of transformational grammar may be found in Appendix F.

This kind of sentence combining, something that can be done without an explicit formal grammar, is explored in Frank O'Hare, *Sentence Combining: Improving Student Writing without Formal Grammar Instruction.*

20. For instance the multi-base deletion transformations in Table 19 show that for the High Group in early years, the male score was 34 and the female score was 37. These two figures added together give the 71 in our table here.

21. See Martin Joos, *The English Verb;* Frank R. Palmer, *A Linguistic Study of the English Verb;* A. F. Watts, *The Language and Mental Development of Children.*

22. Robert L. Allen, *The Verb System of Present-Day American English,* p. 136.

23. Nonfinite verbs are infinitives, participles, and gerunds; finite verbs are those requiring a subject and capable of taking a subject from this list: *it, I, we, you, he, she, they.*

24. One reader of our research has suggested that we may not have used the best measure for verb density. Had we made a *straight count* of verbs, we may have noticed an increase in their use as the subject matured. Since the rest of the communication unit would also increase, however, using percentages would not reflect this increase in verb usage, and might fail to give a true picture. For instance:

Age 6: Norma was petting a stray cat.   2 verbs in 6 words = 30% verbs
Age 10: Our neighbor's pet dog must have   4 verbs in 12 words = 30% verbs
              been fighting an angry wild skunk.

The *number* of verbs increases, but the *percentage* remains the same.

25. William David Green, "A Study of Non-finite Verbs Used by Subjects Differing in Socio-economic Status, Grades 6 and 11" (Ph.D. diss., University of California, Berkeley, 1968).

NOTES TO CHAPTER FIVE

1. For a succinct description of the rhetoric and syntax of cumulative sentences see Walter Loban, Margaret Ryan, and James Squire, *Teaching Language and Literature* (New York: Harcourt, Brace, Jovanovich, 1969), pp. 321-2.

2. The research of both Goldman-Eisler and Lawton is revised,

along with other studies of hesitation phenomena, in Susan Ervin-Tripp and Dan I. Slobin, "Psycholinguistics," *Annual Review of Psychology* 17 (1966): 435-74.

3. Basil Bernstein, "Linguistic Codes, Hesitation Phenomena and Intelligence," *Language and Speech* 5 (1962): 31-46.

4. Denis Lawton, *Social Class, Language, and Education*, p. 107.

5. Walter Loban, *Problems in Oral English*; Walter Loban, *Language Ability: Grades Seven, Eight, and Nine*.

6. Bernard R. Tanner, Craig Vittetoe, and Robert E. Shutes, "Notes on Chapter Five," *English 8, Teachers' Edition, Secondary English Series* (Menlo Park, Calif.: Addison-Wesley Publishing Company, 1968), p. 46.

7. Bernard Tanner, personal letter to Walter Loban.

8. Arnold Gesell and Frances L. Ilg, *The Child from Five to Ten* (New York: Harpers, 1946).

9. Mildred C. Templin, *Certain Language Skills in Children*, Child Welfare Monograph Series No. 26 (Minneapolis: University of Minnesota Press, 1957).

10. Kellogg W. Hunt, *Grammatical Structures Written at Three Grade Levels*.

11. A. F. Watts, *The Language and Mental Development of Children*; Roy C. O'Donnell, William J. Griffin, and Raymond C. Norris, *Syntax of Kindergarten and Elementary School Children*.

12. Courtney B. Cazden, "Evaluation of Learning in Preschool Education: Early Language Development," in *Handbook on Formative and Summative Evaluation of Student Learning*, eds. Benjamin S. Bloom, J. Thomas Hastings, and George F. Madaus (New York: McGraw Hill Book Co., 1971).

13. High Scope, Ypsilanti, Michigan.

14. Far West Laboratory for Educational Development, *Write about a Picture Task* (San Francisco: Far West Laboratory, 1975).

15. Kellogg W. Hunt, "Recent Measures in Syntactic Development," *Elementary English* 43 (1966): 732-9; O'Donnell, Griffin, and Norris, *Syntax of Kindergarten and Elementary School Children*. See especially Chapter IV.

16. Jack McClellan, "Creative Writing Characteristics of Children" (Ph.D. diss., University of South California, Los Angeles, 1956).

17. Basil Bernstein, *Class, Codes and Control: Theoretical Studies in the Sociology of Language*, Vol. 1 (London: Routledge and Kegan Paul, 1971); Millicent Poole, *Social Class Contrasts in Linguistic, Cognitive, and Verbal Domains* (Bundoora, Victoria, Australia: Centre for Urban Studies, La Trobe University, 1975).

18. It also accounts for a misinterpretation in the early years of the study. In our first monograph we reported that every subject knew and used all the basic patterns of the English sentence with the exception of the pattern known as subject–linking verb–predicate nominative (e.g., He is my daddy). We were not sophisticated enough, at that time, to realize that black dialect uses, as does Polish or Russian, a deleted verb *to be* (He my daddy) and does so with no loss of communication or lack of appropriateness in the true linguistic sense. Consequently, in our first monograph we tallied such sentences used by black dialect speakers in the column we called partial sentences rather than in the column for the linking verb pattern. Thus we ended up saying that except for the pattern of the *linking verb* and the use of *partial sentences*, differences between the groups on the basic patterns of the English sentence are not notable (Walter Loban, *The Language of Elementary School Children* [Urbana, Illinois: National Council of Teachers of English, 1963], p. 46). What we should have said is that in the mastery of grammatical sentence patterns there were no significant differences at all. In the long course of this longitudinal research we have learned much about the complexities of black dialect and its effective use of *be*, both in deletion and in accommodating the different durative aspect of the verb as in the following examples:

My daddy working at Sears. (Temporary—He is working there just today.)

My daddy be working at Sears. (Durative—He is working there permanently.)

19. John F. West, "Introduction," in *The Old Man and His Sons*, by Hethin Bra (New York: Paul S. Eriksson, Inc., 1970).

20. Werner Cohn, "On the Language of Lower-Class Children," *School Review* 67 (Winter 1959): 435-40.

NOTES TO APPENDIX B

1. This choice of segmentation is the outcome of a conference sponsored by the U.S. Department of Health, Education, and Welfare at Bloomington, Indiana. The linguistic consultants at this

conference were John Carroll, W. Nelson Francis, Fred House-holder, David Reed, and Harold Whitehall.

2. For a more complete discussion of these terms, see W. Nelson Francis, *The Structure of American English* (New York: Ronald Press, 1958), p. 157. See also Archibald A. Hill, *Introduction to Linguistic Structures* (New York: Harcourt, Brace & World, 1958), pp. 13-30.

3. This is what A. F. Watts calls "the natural linguistic unit." See A. F. Watts, *The Language and Mental Development of Children*, pp. 65-66. See also Kellogg W. Hunt, "A Synopsis of Clause-to-Sentence Length Factors," *English Journal* 54 (1965): 300-309.

4. Walter Loban, *Language Ability: Grades Seven, Eight, and Nine*.

5. Walter Loban, *The Language of Elementary School Children*.

NOTES TO APPENDIX F

1. Walter Loban, *The Language of Elementary School Children*; Kellogg W. Hunt, *Grammatical Structures Written at Three Grade Levels*.

2. Donald R. Bateman and Frank J. Zidonis, *The Effect of a Study of Transformational Grammar on the Writing of Ninth and Tenth Graders*. Research Report No. 6 (Urbana, Ill.: National Council of Teachers of English, 1966); Robert Stockwell, "The Transformational Model of Generative or Predictive Grammar," in *Natural Language and the Computer*, ed. Paul L. Garvin (New York: McGraw-Hill, 1963), pp. 23-46; Paul Roberts, *Modern Grammar* (New York: Harcourt, Brace & World, Inc., 1967).

3. Noam Chomsky, *Aspects of the Theory of Syntax* (Cambridge, Mass.: MIT Press, 1965), pp. 68-74. These notional descriptions sometimes do, by indirection usually, locate the structural *positions* of constituents. Clearly none of Bateman and Zidonis's 46 "transformational rules" are rules at all; they are optional transformations. I think that notional labels are less accurate than categorical or typological descriptions if only because these labels are *vulnerable*: i.e., Is it "obligation" or "causality"? Is the "*object* of the verb" also the "*subject* of the infinitive"? And so on.

4. A question may arise about the presence of *to* and *-ing* in items 6, 7, and 8. Is there a syntactic change here or a morphological one? A similar question occurs in structures like *John + possessive + V-ing* or *his V-ing*; should we search for a syntactic or a nonsyntactic explanation? In the first case I would say that the obligatory rule for tense can be rewritten as *to* or *-ing*, thus obviating the T*ing* and *T del(etion), ing, poss* string that Roberts gets tangled in. Also, in the second case, I think that *John has a hotrod* will produce *John's hotrod* but not *John's hotrodding*, which more likely comes from *John + tense + hotrod ▶ John + poss + -ing + hotrod ▶ John + S + hotrod + ing* . . . (▶ a spelling rule, no doubt). Items 6 and 7 are different enough to require different explanations, it seems to me.

NOTE TO APPENDIX G

1. Pictures 5 and 6 proved to be good stimuli for language. They had been used by Lois Barclay Murphy in her book *Social Behavior and Child Personality* (New York: Columbia University Press, 1937), pp. 193 and 227; Picture 2 was retained for all thirteen years of the study. It appears in Marshall McClintock, *The Story of the Mississippi* (New York: Harper Brothers, 1941), p. 9.